WORD FOR WINDOWS® 95 FOR DUMMIES®

Quick Reference

by Peter Weverka

IDG Books Worldwide, Inc.
An International Data Group Company

Foster City, CA ✦ Chicago, IL ✦ Indianapolis, IN ✦ Southlake, TX

Word For Windows® 95 For Dummies® Quick Reference
Published by
IDG Books Worldwide, Inc.
An International Data Group Company
919 E. Hillsdale Blvd.
Suite 400
Foster City, CA 94404
http://www.idgbooks.com (IDG Books Worldwide Web Site)
http://www.dummies.com (Dummies Press Web Site)

Library of Congress Catalog Card No.: 95-81098

ISBN: 1-56884-980-X

Printed in the United States of America

10 9 8 7 6 5 4 3

1A/SZ/RQ/ZW/IN

Distributed in the United States by IDG Books Worldwide, Inc.

Distributed by Macmillan Canada for Canada; by Contemporanea de Ediciones for Venezuela; by Distribuidora Cuspide for Argentina; by CITEC for Brazil; by Ediciones ZETA S.C.R. Ltda. for Peru; by Editorial Limusa SA for Mexico; by Transworld Publishers Limited in the United Kingdom and Europe; by Academic Bookshop for Egypt; by Levant Distributors S.A.R.L. for Lebanon; by Al Jassim for Saudi Arabia; by Simron Pty. Ltd. for South Africa; by Pustak Mahal for India; by The Computer Bookshop for India; by Toppan Company Ltd. for Japan; by Addison Wesley Publishing Company for Korea; by Longman Singapore Publishers Ltd. for Singapore, Malaysia, Thailand, and Indonesia; by Unalis Corporation for Taiwan; by WS Computer Publishing Company, Inc. for the Philippines; by WoodsLane Pty. Ltd. for Australia; by WoodsLane Enterprises Ltd. for New Zealand. Authorized Sales Agent: Anthony Rudkin Associates for the Middle East and North Africa.

For general information on IDG Books Worldwide's books in the U.S., please call our Consumer Customer Service department at 800-762-2974. For reseller information, including discounts and premium sales, please call our Reseller Customer Service department at 800-434-3422.

For information on where to purchase IDG Books Worldwide's books outside the U.S., please contact our International Sales department at 415-655-3172 or fax 415-655-3295.

For information on foreign language translations, please contact our Foreign & Subsidiary Rights department at 415-655-3021 or fax 415-655-3281.

For sales inquiries and special prices for bulk quantities, please contact our Sales department at 415-655-3200 or write to the address above.

For information on using IDG Books Worldwide's books in the classroom or for ordering examination copies, please contact our Educational Sales department at 800-434-2086 or fax 817-251-8174.

For authorization to photocopy items for corporate, personal, or educational use, please contact Copyright Clearance Center, 222 Rosewood Drive, Danvers, MA 01923, or fax 508-750-4470.

is a trademark under exclusive license to IDG Books Worldwide, Inc., from International Data Group, Inc.

About the Author

Peter Weverka has edited 75 computer books on topics ranging from word processors to desktop publishing to the Internet. He edited about 50 of those books online with Microsoft Word.

Peter wrote one other book, along with Steve Nelson, called *Field Guide to PCs*. His humorous articles and stories (none related to computers, thankfully) have appeared in *Harper's* and *The Corpse*.

Peter believes that the goal of all computing is to help you work faster so you can get away from the office an hour early and take the long, slow, scenic route home.

ABOUT IDG BOOKS WORLDWIDE

Welcome to the world of IDG Books Worldwide.

IDG Books Worldwide, Inc., is a subsidiary of International Data Group, the world's largest publisher of computer-related information and the leading global provider of information services on information technology. IDG was founded more than 25 years ago and now employs more than 7,700 people worldwide. IDG publishes more than 250 computer publications in 67 countries (see listing below). More than 70 million people read one or more IDG publications each month.

Launched in 1990, IDG Books Worldwide is today the #1 publisher of best-selling computer books in the United States. We are proud to have received 8 awards from the Computer Press Association in recognition of editorial excellence and three from Computer Currents' First Annual Readers' Choice Awards, and our best-selling ...For Dummies® series has more than 19 million copies in print with translations in 28 languages. IDG Books Worldwide, through a joint venture with IDG's Hi-Tech Beijing, became the first U.S. publisher to publish a computer book in the People's Republic of China. In record time, IDG Books Worldwide has become the first choice for millions of readers around the world who want to learn how to better manage their businesses.

Our mission is simple: Every one of our books is designed to bring extra value and skill-building instructions to the reader. Our books are written by experts who understand and care about our readers. The knowledge base of our editorial staff comes from years of experience in publishing, education, and journalism — experience which we use to produce books for the '90s. In short, we care about books, so we attract the best people. We devote special attention to details such as audience, interior design, use of icons, and illustrations. And because we use an efficient process of authoring, editing, and desktop publishing our books electronically, we can spend more time ensuring superior content and spend less time on the technicalities of making books.

You can count on our commitment to deliver high-quality books at competitive prices on topics you want to read about. At IDG Books Worldwide, we continue in the IDG tradition of delivering quality for more than 25 years. You'll find no better book on a subject than one from IDG Books Worldwide.

John J. Kilcullen

John Kilcullen
President and CEO
IDG Books Worldwide, Inc.

IDG Books Worldwide, Inc., is a subsidiary of International Data Group, the world's largest publisher of computer-related information and the leading global provider of information services on information technology. International Data Group publishes over 250 computer publications in 67 countries. Seventy million people read one or more International Data Group publications each month. International Data Group's publications include: ARGENTINA: Computerworld Argentina, GamePro, Infoworld, PC World Argentina; AUSTRALIA: Australian Macworld, Client/Server Journal, Computer Living, Computerworld, Digital News, Network World, PC World, Publishing Essentials, Reseller; AUSTRIA: Computerwelt, PC TEST; BELARUS: PC World Belarus; BELGIUM: Data News, BRAZIL: Annuário de Informática, Computerworld Brazil, Connections, Super Game Power, Macworld, PC World Brazil, Publish Brazil, SUPERGAME; BULGARIA: Computerworld Bulgaria, Networkworld/Bulgaria, PC & MacWorld Bulgaria; CANADA: CIO Canada, ComputerWorld Canada, InfoCanada, Network World Canada, Reseller World; CHILE: Computerworld Chile, GamePro, PC World Chile; COLUMBIA: Computerworld Colombia, GamePro, PC World Colombia; COSTA RICA: PC World Costa Rica/Nicaragua; THE CZECH AND SLOVAK REPUBLICS: Computerworld Czechoslovakia, Elektronika Czechoslovakia, PC World Czechoslovakia; DENMARK: Communications World, Computerworld Danmark, Macworld Danmark, PC World Danmark, PC World Danmark Supplements, TECH World; DOMINICAN REPUBLIC: PC World Republica Dominicana; ECUADOR: PC World Ecuador, GamePro; EGYPT: Computerworld Middle East, PC World Middle East; EL SALVADOR: PC World Centro America; FINLAND: MikroPC, Tietoverkko, Tietoviikko; FRANCE: Distributique, Golden, Info PC, Le Guide du Monde Informatique, Le Monde Informatique, Reseaux & Telecoms; GERMANY: Computer Business, Computerwoche, Computerwoche Extra, Computerwoche Focus, Electronic Entertainment, GamePro, I/M Information Management, Macwelt, PC Welt; GREECE: GamePro, Macworld & Publish; GUATEMALA: PC World Centro America; HONDURAS: PC World Centro America; HONG KONG: Computerworld Hong Kong, PCWorld Hong Kong, Publish in Asia; HUNGARY: ABCD CD-ROM, Computerworld Szamitastechnika, PC & Mac World Hungary, PC-X Magazine; INDIA: Computerworld India, PC World India, Publish in Asia; INDONESIA: InfoKomputer PC World, Komputek Computerworld, Publish in Asia; IRELAND: ComputerScope, PC Live!; ISRAEL: PC World 32 BIT, People & Computers; ITALY: Computerworld Italia, Computerworld Italia Special Editions, Lotus Italia, Macworld Italia, Networking Italia, PC Shopping, PC World Italia, PC World/Walt Disney; JAPAN: Macworld Japan, Nikkei Personal Computing, SunWorld Japan, Windows World Japan; KENYA: East African Computer News; KOREA: Hi-Tech Information/Computerworld, Macworld Korea, PC World Korea; MACEDONIA: PC World Macedonia; MALAYSIA: Computerworld Malaysia, PC World Malaysia, Publish in Asia; MEXICO: Computerworld Mexico, GamePro, Macworld, PC World Mexico; MYANMAR: PC World Myanmar; NETHERLANDS: Computable, Computer! Totaal, LAN Magazine, Macworld, Net Magazine; NEW ZEALAND: Computer Buyer, Computerworld New Zealand, MTB, Network World, PC World New Zealand; NICARAGUA: PC World Costa Rica/Nicaragua; NIGERIA: PC World Africa; NORWAY: Computerworld Norge, Computerworld Privat, CW Rapport Klient/Tjener, CW Rapport Nettverk & Telecom, CW Rapport Offentlig Sektor, IDG's KURSGUIDE, Macworld Norge, Multimedia World, PC World Ekspress, PC World Nettverk, PC World Norge, PC World's Produktguide, Windows Spesial; PAKISTAN: Computerworld Pakistan, PC World Pakistan; PANAMA: GamePro, PC World Panama; PARAGUAY: PC World Paraguay; P. R. OF CHINA: China Computerworld, China Infoworld, Computer & Communication, Electronic Product World, Electronics Today, Game Camp, PC World China, Popular Computer Week, Software World, Telecom Product World; PERU: Computerworld Peru, GamePro, PC World Professional Peru, PC World Peru; POLAND: Computerworld Poland, Computerworld Special Report, Macworld, Networld, PC World Komputer; PHILIPPINES: Computerworld Philippines, PC Digest, Publish in Asia; PORTUGAL: Cerebro/PC World, Correio Informático/Computerworld, Mac•In/PC•In Portugal; PUERTO RICO: PC World Puerto Rico; ROMANIA: Computerworld Romania, PC World Romania, Telecom Romania; RUSSIA: Computerworld Rossiya, Network World Russia, PC World Russia; SINGAPORE: Computerworld Singapore, PC World Singapore, Publish in Asia; SLOVENIA: MONITOR; SOUTH AFRICA: Computing S.A., Network World S.A., Software World; SPAIN: Computerworld España, COMUNICACIONES WORLD, Dealer World, Macworld España, PC World España; SWEDEN: CAP&Design, Computer Sweden, Corporate Computing, Macworld, Maxi Data, MikroDatorn, Närverk & Kommunikation, PC/Aktiv, PC World, Windows World; SWITZERLAND: Computerworld Schweiz, Macworld Schweiz, PCtip, Publish in Asia; TURKEY: Computerworld Monitör, MACWORLD Turkiye, PC WORLD Turkiye; UKRAINE: Computerworld Kiev, Computers & Software Magazine, PC World Ukraine; UNITED KINGDOM: Acorn User, Amiga Action, Amiga Computing, Amiga, Appletalk, CD Powerplay, CD-ROM Now, Computing, Connexion, GamePro, Lotus Magazine, Macaction, Macworld, Open Computing, Parents and Computers, PC Home, PC Works, The WEB; UNITED STATES: Cable in the Classroom, CD Review, CIO Magazine, Computerworld, Computerworld Client/Server Journal, Digital Video Magazine, DOS World, Electronic, InfoWorld, I-Way, Macworld, Maximize, MULTIMEDIA WORLD, Network World, PC World, PUBLISH, SWATPro Magazine, Video Event, WebMaster; URUGUAY: PC World Uruguay; VENEZUELA: Computerworld Venezuela, GamePro, PC World Venezuela; and VIETNAM: PC World Vietnam

IDG BOOKS WORLDWIDE

Dedication

For Ethel and Bob.

Acknowledgments

This book owes a lot to a lot of different people. I am especially grateful to former Acquisitions Editor Megg Bonar, who offered me the opportunity to write this book, and to Steve Nelson of the Great Northwest, who told Megg that I could write a good book about Word 95.

I also wish to thank Pam Mourouzis, who served as project editor and copy editor and was very cheerful about the whole undertaking, and Tammy Castleman, who copyedited part of the manuscript. In today's worldwide copy editor shortage, I count myself very lucky to have had such capable editors.

Thanks as well go to technical editor Ray Werner, who made sure that every task in this book is indeed explained correctly, and to Steve Rath, who wrote a superb index.

I also owe a debt to these people at IDG who had a hand in my book: Milissa Koloski, Diane Steele, Kristin Cocks, Judi Taylor, Kathy Cox, Colleen Rainsberger, Julie King, Suki Gear, Melissa Buddendeck, Beth Jenkins, Sherry Gomoll, Angie Hunckler, and the rest of the Production team.

Finally, my heartfelt thanks to Sofia, Henry, and Addie for indulging me.

Publisher's Acknowledgments

We're proud of this book; send us your comments about it by using the Reader Response Card at the back of the book or by e-mailing us at feedback/dummies@idgbooks.com. Some of the people who helped bring this book to market include:

Acquisitions, Development, and Editorial

Project Editor: Pamela Mourouzis

Assistant Acquisitions Editor: Gareth Hancock

Product Development Manager: Mary Bednarek

Copy Editor: Tamara S. Castleman

Technical Reviewer: Ray Werner

Editorial Managers: Kristin A. Cocks, Mary C. Corder

Editorial Assistants: Constance Carlisle, Chris Collins

Production

Project Coordinator: Sherry Gomoll

Layout and Graphics: E. Shawn Aylsworth, Angela F. Hunckler, Todd Klemme, Jill Lyttle, Carla Radzikinas, Gina Scott

Proofreaders: Melissa D. Buddendeck, Gwenette Gaddis, Dwight Ramsey, Carl Saff, Robert Springer

Indexer: Steve Rath

General and Administrative

IDG Books Worldwide, Inc.: John Kilcullen, President and CEO; Steven Berkowitz, COO and Publisher

Dummies, Inc.: Milissa Koloski, Executive Vice President and Publisher

Dummies Technology Press and Dummies Editorial: Diane Graves Steele, Vice President and Associate Publisher; Judith A. Taylor, Brand Manager

Dummies Trade Press: Kathleen A. Welton, Vice President and Publisher; Stacy S. Collins, Brand Manager

IDG Books Production for Dummies Press: Beth Jenkins, Production Director; Cindy L. Phipps, Supervisor of Project Coordination; Kathie S. Schutte, Supervisor of Page Layout; Shelley Lea, Supervisor of Graphics and Design; Debbie J. Gates, Production Systems Specialist; Tony Augsburger, Reprint Coordinator; Leslie Popplewell, Media Archive Coordinator

Dummies Packaging and Book Design: Patti Sandez, Packaging Assistant; Kavish+Kavish, Cover Design

♦

The publisher would like to give special thanks to Patrick J. McGovern, without whom this book would not have been possible.

♦

Table of Contents

Intro: How to Use This Book 1

What's in This Book, Anyway? 2
The Cast of Icons 2
Conventions Used in This Book 3
Give Me Your Two Cents' Worth! 4

Part I: Getting to Know Word 95 5

Cursors, Cursors, and More Cursors 6
What Is a Document? 6
The Keyboard 7
Using the Mouse 9
Making Menu Choices 9
    Shortcut keys for doing it quickly 10
    Those mysterious shortcut menus 10
Filling In a Dialog Box 11
What All That Stuff On-Screen Is 12
Understanding How Paragraphs Work 14
Starting Word 95 15
Introducing Windows 95 16
    Changing the size of the Word 95 window 16
    Switching applications with the taskbar 16

Part II: Setting Up and Editing a Document 17

Breaking a Line 18
Breaking a Page 18
Changing the Look of the Screen 19
Changing lowercase to UPPERCASE,
UPPERCASE to lowercase 20
Closing a Document 22
Copying, Moving, and Pasting Text 22
Dashes 24
Deleting Text 24
Exiting Word 95 25
Finding and Replacing Text and Formats 25
Finding the Right Word with the Thesaurus 26
Finding Text and More 27
Getting the Help You Need 29
Grammar-Checking Your Document 30
Hyphenating a Document 31
    Hyphenating a paragraph manually 32
    Unhyphenating and other hyphenation tasks 33
Inserting a Whole File in a Document 34
Moving Around in Documents 34
Numbering the Pages 36

Opening an Existing Document 38
Opening a New Document 38
Putting Headers and Footers on Pages 39
Saving a Document for the First Time 40
Saving a Document under a New Name 41
Saving a Document You've Been Working On 42
Selecting Text in Speedy Ways 43
Spacing Lines 43
Spell-Checking Your Document 45
Symbols and Special Characters 46
Undoing a Mistake 47
Viewing Documents in Different Ways 48
Working on Many Documents at Once.. 49
Working in Two Places in the Same Document 50
    Opening a second window 50
    Splitting the screen 51
Zooming In and Zooming Out 52

Part III: Formatting Documents and Text 53

Adding Bold, Italic, Underline, and Other Styles 54
Centering, Justifying, and Aligning Text 55
Changing the Font of Text 56
Creating Numbered and Bulleted Lists 57
Dividing a Document into Sections 59
Dropping In a Drop Cap 60
Formatting a Document 61
    Fast formatting with the Format Painter 62
    Using styles for consistent formatting 62
    Using styles from the Style Gallery 67
    Formatting a document automatically.................................... 68
Indenting Paragraphs and First Lines 69
Numbering the Headings in a Document 72
Numbering the Lines in a Document... 73
Putting Newspaper-Style Columns in a Document 74
Setting Up and Changing the Margins 77
Working with the Ruler 78
Working with Tabs 79

Part IV: Printing Your Documents 81

Previewing What You Print 82
Printing Addresses on Envelopes 83
Printing on Different-Sized Paper 85
Printing a Document 86
Printing Labels 87
    Printing labels one at a time 88
    Printing labels for mass mailings 89
Solving Problems with the Printer 93
Telling Word 95 How to Print Documents 94

Part V: Making Your Work Go Faster 95

Bookmarks for Hopping Around 96
Correcting Typos on the Fly 97
Customizing Word 95 99
    Changing the menu commands 99
    Changing the keyboard shortcuts 101
Entering Graphics and Text Quickly 102
Entering Information Quickly with Forms 103
Form(ing) Letters 106
Going Here, Going There in Documents 110
Inserting Automatic Information in Documents 111
Linking Documents to Save on Work 112
    Creating a link 112
    Updating, breaking, and changing links 113
Macros 115
    Recording a macro 115
    Running a macro 116
    Deleting a macro 117
Master Documents for Really Big Jobs 117
    Creating a new master document 118
    Assembling documents for a master document 118
    Removing, moving, locking, splitting, merging,
       and renaming subdocuments 120
Outlines for Organizing Your Work 121
Rearranging the Toolbars 123
    Displaying other toolbars 123
    Putting your own buttons on toolbars 124
    Creating your own toolbar 126
Repeating an Action — and Quicker This Time 127
Searching with Wildcards 128

Part VI: Desktop Publishing 129

Anchoring Text and Graphics 130
Bordering and Shading Paragraphs and Graphics 131
Coloring Text 134
Constructing the Perfect Table 135
    Creating a table 136
    Entering text in a table 137
    Changing the layout of a table 138
    Formatting a table 143
    Repeating header rows on subsequent pages 146
    Merging and splitting cells and tables 146
    Using math formulas in tables 146
Drawing in Word 95 147
Fixing Spacing Problems in Headings 148
Inserting a Frame for Text or a Graphic 149
    Inserting the frame 149
    Changing and moving the frame 150

Inserting Pictures and Graphics in Documents 153
Putting text inside a graphic 154
Cropping a graphic 155
Keeping Paragraphs and Lines Together 155
"Landscape" Documents 157
Making Room to Bind a Document 158

Part VII: Fancy and Esoteric Stuff 159

Annotating a Document 160
Creating a Table of Figures, Tables, or Equations 161
Generating a Table of Contents 163
Hidden Text and Secret Messages 165
Including a Database in a Document 166
Indexing a Document 168
Marking index items in the document 168
Generating an index 171
Editing an index 173
Keeping Track of Document Revisions 173
Marking your revisions 174
Comparing and merging documents 175
Accepting and rejecting revisions 176
Putting Captions on Figures and Tables 176
Putting Cross-References in a Document 178
Putting Footnotes and Endnotes in Documents 179
Inserting a footnote or endnote 180
Changing the numbering scheme and position of notes 181
Deleting, moving, and editing notes 182

Part VIII: Potpourri 183

Backing Up Your Work 184
Backing up to a floppy disk or tape drive 184
Backing up files in Word 95 185
Restoring a backup copy of a file 186
Finding a Missing File 187
Getting Information about a Document 188
Highlighting Parts of a Document 190
Importing and Exporting Files 190
Importing a file 190
Exporting a file 191
Including Video Clips and Sound in Documents 191
Protecting Your Work with Passwords 192
Keeping others from opening a file 192
Opening a password-protected file 194
Removing a password 194
Keeping others from changing a file 194
Protecting parts of a document from changes 195
Tips for Learning Word 196

Glossary: Techie Talk *197*

Index *201*

How to Use This Book

Keep this book on the corner of your desk. When you want to try something new, want to try something you're unsure of, or tell yourself that *there has to be a better way,* open this book, and I'll tell you what it is and how to do it.

This little book cannot cover every nook and cranny of Microsoft Word for Windows 95, but it covers the fundamental things that everybody needs to know. And it gives you enough instruction so that you can get going on the complicated things.

Over the years, I've discovered a lot of shortcuts and tricks for using this program. I've thrown them into the mix, too, so you can be the beneficiary of my many years of blind groping and daring experimentation.

What's in This Book, Anyway?

To find what you're looking for in this book, your best bet is to go to the index or the table of contents. Other than that, I've organized this book into eight parts, and I invite you to browse in one part or another until you find what you need.

+ Part I describes basic techniques and translates ugly word processing jargon into modern American English.

+ Part II explains the editing tasks that everyone who wants to use this program wisely should know. You'll find a lot of shortcuts in Part II.

+ Part III describes formatting. A document communicates by its words but also by the way it is laid out. In Part III, I tell you how to format a document so that readers will know exactly what you're all about just by glancing at the page.

+ In Part IV, I explain printing. When you can't print things correctly, it's a nightmare. I hope you never have to visit Part IV.

+ Part V tells you how to make your work go faster. If you're going to browse, browse in Part V. You'll discover things that you wouldn't think to look for on your own.

+ Part VI sort of picks up where Part III left off. In many ways, Word 95 is more of a desktop publishing program than a word processing program. Part VI looks at Word's desktop publishing features.

+ Part VII delves into the fancy and the esoteric. It explains cross-references, footnotes, tables of contents, and other things of use to people who create complex documents.

+ Part VIII is a hodgepodge conglomeration of the strange and useful. It explains how to back up documents, find missing files, and see how many minutes you've worked on a document, among other things.

+ After all the parts is a short glossary of computer terms. If you need to know what *cursor, field, cell,* and other peculiar terms mean, have a look in the Glossary.

The Cast of Icons

To help you get more out of this book, I've placed icons here and there. Here's what the icons mean:

Microsoft Weird 95 has a few odd features and quirks. You can't spell words certain ways without being "AutoCorrected," for example. Try entering a lowercase letter after a period — you can't do it. Word does weird things because it makes a lot of assumptions about what the typical user wants. You, however, may not be a typical user. When I describe the weird things that Word does, I'll put a Weirdness icon in the margin.

 Of course, Word 95 has a lot of great stuff, too. I'm sure you know that, or else you wouldn't be using the program. Where I describe Word's most wonderful, speedy, advantageous, effective, and powerful features (I'm getting these adjectives from the Thesaurus), I'll put a Cool Stuff icon in the margin.

 Next to the Tip icon, you'll find shortcuts and tricks of the trade.

 Where you see this icon, tread softly and carefully. It means that you are opening Pandora's box or doing something you might regret later.

 In Word 95, there are usually two ways to do everything: the fast but dicey way and the slow but thorough way. When I explain how to do a task the fast way, I'll put a Fast Track icon in the margin.

 If you need more information than this book provides, look for these icons. They tell you which topics are covered in more detail in *Word For Windows 95 For Dummies* (IDG Books Worldwide, Inc.) or some other *...For Dummies* book.

Conventions Used in This Book

To make using this book easier for you, I've adopted a few conventions.

 Where I tell you to click a button, a picture of the button appears in the left-hand margin. For example, the button you see here is the Save button. Where I tell you to "click the Save button to save your document," you'll see the Save button out to the left so that you know exactly which button to click.

Besides clicking buttons, you can do tasks in Word 95 by pressing combinations of keys. For example, you can save a document by pressing Ctrl+S. In other words, you press the Ctrl key and the S key at the same time. Where you see Ctrl+, Alt+, or Shift+ and a key name (or maybe more than one key name), press the keys simultaneously.

To show you how to issue commands, I use the ⇨ symbol. For example, you can choose File⇨Save to save a document. The ⇨ is just a shorthand method of saying, "Choose Save from the File menu."

Notice how the *F* in *File* and the *S* in *Save* are underlined in the preceding paragraph. Those same characters are underlined in the command names in Word 95. Underlined letters are called *hot keys*. You can press them to give commands and make selections in dialog boxes. Where a letter is underlined in a command name or in a dialog box in Word 95, it is also underlined in this book.

Step-by-step directions in this book are numbered to make them easier to follow. When you're doing a task, do it by the numbers. Sometimes, however, you have to make choices in order to give a command. When you have to make a choice in a dialog box or you have different options for completing a task, I present the choices in a bulleted list. For example, here are the three ways to begin spell-checking a document:

+ Choose Tools⇨Spelling.

+ Press F7.

+ Click the Spelling button.

Where you see words or letters in boldface text in this book, I want you to type the letters. For example, if you read, "Type **annual report.doc** in the File name text box to name your document," you should do just that. Type those very same letters.

Give Me Your Two Cents' Worth!

Best of luck, reader. Every trick I know for getting the most out of Word 95 is in this book. If you've discovered a trick of your own and would like to share it with me, I would be most grateful. Please e-mail it to me at 74364.50@compuserve.com. I'll include it in the next edition of this book and even put your name in lights in the Acknowledgments.

Part 1

Getting to Know Word 95

If you've been around word processors for a while, you needn't read this part of the book. But if you haven't used a word processor before, read on. I'll tell you what mysterious words like *cursor, double-click,* and *scroll* mean. I'll give you the basics so that you can get going with Word 95.

If you just started using Windows 95, you might want to take a peek at "Introducing Windows 95," the last topic in this part.

In this part...

✔ **What a document is, exactly**

✔ **What the cursor and the other weird stuff on-screen are**

✔ **Making menu choices and filling in a dialog box**

✔ **Using the mouse**

✔ **Finding your way around in Windows 95**

What Is a Document?

Document is just a fancy name for a letter, report, announcement, or proclamation that you create with Word.

When you first start Word 95, you see a document with the generic name "Document1." But if you already have a document on-screen and want to start a new one, click the New button, shown at left. A brand-new document with the generic name "Document2" in the title bar opens. (The *title bar* is the stripe across the top of the computer screen.) It's called "Document 2" because it's the second one you're working on. The document keeps that name until you save it and give it a name of your own.

Say you decide to call your first document "First." When you save it (by clicking the Save button or choosing File⊃Save) and give it the name "First" in the Save As dialog box, Word renames it "First.doc." The *.doc* at the end of the name stands for *document*. Word 95 documents always have a *.doc* ending, called a *file extension,* so you know what they are.

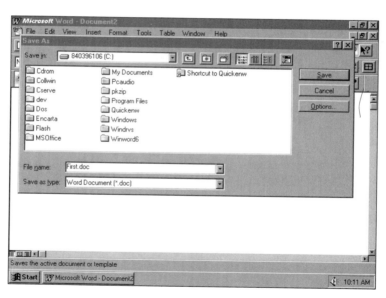

Cursors, Cursors, and More Cursors

Cursors are little symbols that let you know where you are on-screen or what the computer is doing. There are a bunch of different cursors, but the only ones you really need to know about are listed in the following table:

Cursor	What It Does
Insertion point	Sits in the text and blinks on and off. All the action takes place at the insertion point. When you start typing, text appears where the insertion point is. When you paste something from the Clipboard, it appears at the insertion point.
Mouse cursor	Moves around on-screen when you move your mouse. Jiggle your mouse to see what the mouse cursor is. When it's over something that you can select — a menu item or button, for example — it turns into an arrow. Click the mouse when it's an arrow to select a menu item or press a button. When the mouse cursor is over text, it looks like a large, egotistical *I*. To enter text in a new place, move the *I*, click, and start typing.
Help cursor	Click the Help button and drag the Help cursor to the part of the screen you want to know more about. When you click, Word 95 shows you a Help screen with instructions for using the thing you clicked.
Busy cursor	When Word 95 is really busy, you see an hourglass on-screen. Twiddle your thumbs until the hourglass disappears, and then get back to work.

The Keyboard

Most of the keys on the keyboard are probably familiar to you, but what are those weird keys camping out on the edges? Start in the upper-left corner of the keyboard and proceed clockwise:

Key (s)	What It Does
Esc	Backs you out of whatever you're doing. If you pull down a menu or dialog box but are frightened by what you see, you can always press Esc to get out.
F1–F12	These are called *function keys*. You press them alone or in combination with the Ctrl and Shift keys to get various things done quickly.
Print Screen, Scroll Lock, and Pause	These keys are like the human appendix. They were good for something in the computer's evolutionary past, but now they just take up space on the keyboard.
Insert	When you type, the letters you enter push aside the letters that are already there. But if you press Insert, the letters you type cover the other letters. This key also appears on the numeric keypad, where it is called Ins and shares space with the zero. (The *numeric keypad* is the assortment of number keys on the right side of the keyboard.)

(continued)

Key (s)	What It Does
Home	Pressing Home moves the insertion point to the left margin. A second Home key, which does the same thing as the first Home key, appears on the numeric keypad.
Page Up	Press this key to move the insertion point up in the document. It goes up by the length of one computer screen. You'll also find this key on the numeric keypad, along with the number 9, where it has the hiccuppy name PgUp.
Enter	A very important key. Press it to end a paragraph in Word or to say "okay" to the settings in a dialog box.
Delete	Press this key to remove characters at the insertion point. You can also select sentences, paragraphs, or even whole pages and press Delete to remove gobs of text in one mighty blow. On the numeric keypad, this key is called Del.
End	Moves the insertion point to the end of a line of text. It is also on the numeric keypad.
Page Down	Moves the insertion point downward in a document by the length of one computer screen. This key also appears on the numeric keypad along with the number 3.
Num Lock	Press Num Lock to make the keys on the numeric keypad act like number keys instead of direction keys. If you're seeing numbers on-screen and want to move the insertion point instead, Num Lock is on when it shouldn't be. Press Num Lock again to make the keys on the numeric keypad act like direction keys.
← ↑ → and ↓	These arrow keys, which share space on the numeric keypad with the 4, 8, 6, and 2 keys, respectively, move the insertion point left, up, right, and down on-screen. You'll find another set of arrow keys at the bottom of the keyboard, between the numeric keypad and the Ctrl key.
Ctrl	The Control key. Press this one along with function keys and letter keys to make Word work quickly. For example, the fastest way to save a document is to press Ctrl+S.
Alt	The Alternate key. Like Ctrl, this is another cattle prod to get Word to do things quickly. Press Alt and one of the underlined letters on the main menu to pull down a menu when you're in a hurry.
Shift	Press this key and a letter to get a capital letter instead of a measly lowercase one.
Caps Lock	Someday soon, you'll be typing along AND DARN IT, YOU'LL START GETTING ALL CAPITAL LETTERS. That's because you accidentally pressed the Caps Lock key. Press it again to go back to lowercase, or press it if you *want* to type ALL UPPERCASE letters.

Using the Mouse

The *mouse* is the thing you roll across the desk to make the mouse cursor move across your screen. It is called a mouse because the skinny cord that connects it to your computer looks like a mouse's tail. Originally, it was going to be called the *rat,* but someone got squeamish.

The mouse has two buttons. You usually click the left button, although clicking the right one has advantages, too. Try clicking the right button on a part of the screen you're curious about, for example. You'll sometimes see a *shortcut menu* — a list of menu options that pertain to the part of the screen you clicked.

Often, you are asked to *click* the mouse on menu items, icons, and text. When you're asked to click the mouse, click the left mouse button. Only click the right button if you are specifically told to.

You'll do a lot of clicking around in Word. The following table gives you the lowdown on *click* terminology:

Click	What It Means or Does
click	Press the left mouse button quickly.
right-click	Press the right mouse button quickly.
Shift+click	Click the left mouse button while holding down the Shift key.
Ctrl+click	Click the left mouse button while holding down the Ctrl key.
double-click	Press the left mouse button twice — and do it quickly, as though your life depended on it.
click and drag	Press the mouse button and, while still holding it down, drag the mouse over some text. *Dragging* the mouse just means to roll it across your screen. Clicking and dragging is the fastest way to select text.

Making Menu Choices

To do things in Word, you click a button, press a shortcut key combination, or choose an option from a menu.

At the top of the screen is a list of menus called the *main menu:*

To *pull down* a menu from this list, you can either click the menu name or press the Alt key and the letter that is underlined in the menu name. For example, to pull down the File menu, you can either click the word File or press Alt+F. When you do, a *pull-down menu* appears as if by magic.

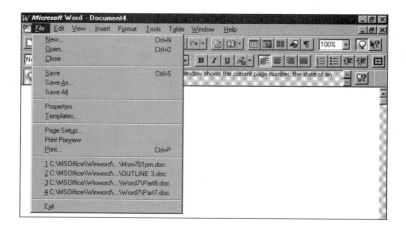

Now you have several *menu commands* to choose from. To choose a command from a pull-down menu, either click the command name or press the letter that is underlined in the command name. Suppose you want to choose the Open command in the File menu. After the File menu drops down, you can either click the word *Open* or press the letter *O* on your keyboard to open a new document.

Shortcut keys for doing it quickly

Notice that some commands on the File menu have Ctrl+key combinations next to their names. These are called *shortcut keys*. If you want to open a new document, for example, you can just press Ctrl+O, the shortcut key combination for opening a document.

Lots of menu commands have shortcut keys that help you get your work done faster. If you find yourself using a command often, see if it has a shortcut key and start using the shortcut key to save time.

You may also notice that some menu commands have ellipses (three dots) next to their names. When you choose one of these commands, a dialog box appears on-screen. *See* "Filling In a Dialog Box" a bit further ahead for more information about dialog boxes.

Those mysterious shortcut menus

Shortcut menus are mysterious little menus that sometimes pop up when you click the right mouse button. For example, you get this shortcut menu when you click the right mouse button in the middle of a document:

These are basic editing commands for working on a document.

When you right-click a word with a squiggly red line underneath it, you see a shortcut menu with suggestions for correcting your misspelled word:

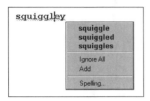

Filling In a Dialog Box

When Word needs a lot of information to complete a command, a *dialog box* appears on-screen. You have to fill out the dialog box before Word will do what you ask it to do. Here is the dialog box you get when you ask Word to print a document, for example:

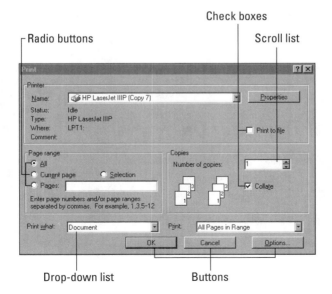

At the bottom is a *drop-down list.* Click the arrow that points down, and down comes a list of such things as annotations and summary information that you can print in addition to the document itself.

Notice the Number of copies *scroll list.* Click the little arrow that points up, and the number climbs so that you can print two, three, four, or more copies. Click the down-pointing arrow to get back to four, three, two, and one copy.

Four *radio buttons* tell Word which part of the document to print. The thing to know about radio buttons is that you can choose only one, just like you can only listen to "Super Country KCOW" or "Rockin' KROQ," but not both stations at once. In this dialog box, you can print the whole document, the page the cursor is in, a selection of text, or a range of pages.

At the bottom of the Print dialog box are some buttons. All dialog boxes have an OK button and a Cancel button. Click OK (or press the Enter key) after you fill out the dialog box and are ready for Word to execute the command. Click Cancel if you lose your nerve and want to start all over again.

Notice the two *check boxes* in the Print dialog box. Check boxes work like radio buttons, except you can select more than one or none at all.

Some dialog boxes have *tabs,* which you click to get another page of settings. For example, the Options dialog box has a grand total of 12 tabs. If you want to change how Word saves documents, click the Save tab. To change the view settings, click the View tab. Choose Tools⇨Options to see the dialog box (on the next page).

What All That Stuff On-Screen Is

Seeing the Word 95 screen for the first time is sort of like trying to find your way through Tokyo's busy Ikebukuro subway station. It's intimidating. But once you start using Word 95, you'll quickly learn what everything is. In the meantime, the following table gives you some shorthand descriptions.

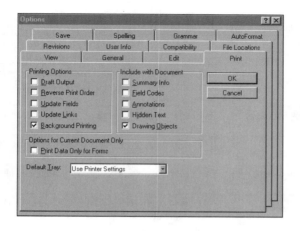

Format bar
Toolbar
Control menu
Title bar   Document window   Menu bar   Ruler
Document window buttons
Minimize, Maximize, and Close buttons

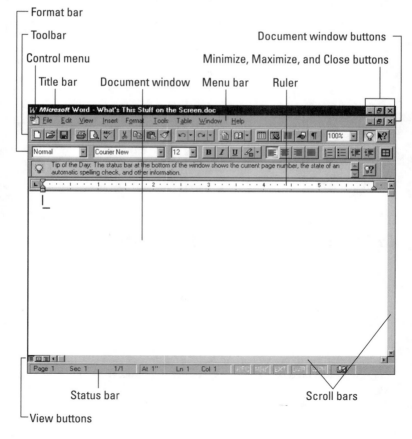

Status bar
Scroll bars
View buttons

Part of Screen	What It Is
Title bar	At the top of the screen, the title bar tells you the name of the document you're working on.
Control menu	Click here to pull down a menu with options for minimizing, maximizing, moving, and closing the window.
Minimize, Maximize, Close buttons	These three magic buttons make it very easy to shrink, enlarge, and close the window.
Menu bar	Choose from this list of main menu options, from File to Help, to give Word 95 commands.
Document window buttons	Click these buttons to shrink, enlarge, and close the document window.
Toolbar	Offers buttons that you can click to execute Word 95 commands.
Format bar	Offers formatting buttons and pull-down lists for changing the appearance of text.
Document window	Here you do the real work of writing words and laying out text.
Ruler	The ruler tells you how wide your margins are, among other things.
Scroll bars	The scroll bars help you move around in a document. See "Moving Around in Documents" in Part II to learn how to use them.
View buttons	Click one of these to change your view of a document.
Status bar	Here's where you can get basic information about where you are and what you're doing in a document. The status bar tells you what page and what section you're in, the total number of pages in the document, where the insertion point is on the page, and the time.

Understanding How Paragraphs Work

Back in English class, your teacher taught you that a paragraph is a part of a longer composition that presents one idea or, in the case of dialogue, presents the words of one speaker. Your teacher was right, too, but for word processing purposes, a paragraph is a lot less than that. In word processing, a paragraph is simply what you put on-screen before you press the Enter key.

For instance, a heading is a paragraph. So is a graphic. If you press Enter on a blank line to go to the next line, the blank line is considered a paragraph. If you type *Dear John* at the top of a letter and press Enter, "Dear John" is a paragraph.

It's important to know this because paragraphs have a lot to do with formatting. If you choose the Format⇨Paragraph command and monkey around with the paragraph formatting, all your changes affect everything in the paragraph that contains the cursor. To make format changes to a whole paragraph, all you have to do is place the cursor there. You don't have to select the paragraph.

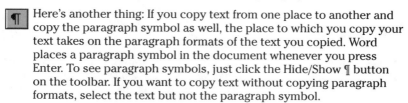 Here's another thing: If you copy text from one place to another and copy the paragraph symbol as well, the place to which you copy your text takes on the paragraph formats of the text you copied. Word places a paragraph symbol in the document whenever you press Enter. To see paragraph symbols, just click the Hide/Show ¶ button on the toolbar. If you want to copy text without copying paragraph formats, select the text but not the paragraph symbol.

Starting Word 95

In Windows 95, all you have to do to start Word is this:

1. Click the Start button on the taskbar.

2. Choose Programs.

3. Choose Microsoft Office.

4. Choose Microsoft Word.

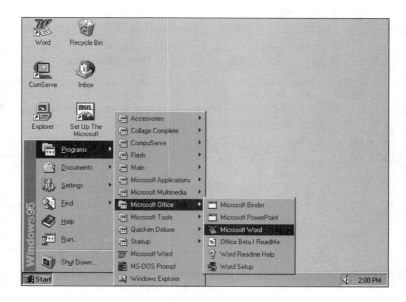

 By the way, if all that clicking to start Word strains your wrist, you should know that you can put a shortcut icon on the desktop next to the My Computer and Recycle Bin icons and start Word merely by clicking its icon. Or you can set things up so that Word starts whenever you turn on your computer. Get a good book like Andy Rathbone's *Windows 95 For Dummies* (IDG Books Worldwide, Inc.) to find out how.

Introducing Windows 95

Windows 95 is the monolithic new operating system from Microsoft. It has everything in it *including* the kitchen sink, so a little book like this can't possibly do it justice. Here, I'll just give you the basics and tell you the most important things that changed from Windows 3.*x*. To get all the dope on Windows 95, read *Windows 95 For Dummies*.

Changing the size of the Word 95 window

When you click the *W* on the left end of the title bar, you see the Control menu. It offers commands for working with the Microsoft Word 95 program window:

Gone are the old Minimize and Maximize buttons of Windows 3.*x*, and in their place are three buttons on the right side of the title bar:

✦ The new Minimize button makes Word 95 disappear from the screen. But the program is still running. To see the Word screen again after you click the Minimize button, click Microsoft Word on the taskbar.

✦ Click the Minimize/Restore button to make the Word window smaller. When you shrink the screen, the button changes into a square. Click the square Restore button again to make Word 95 window fill the screen.

✦ Click the Close button to shut down Word 95. You can also close the program by choosing File⇨Exit.

Switching applications with the taskbar

Along the bottom of the screen is the *taskbar,* which allows you to run a bunch of applications at once. The names of all the applications that are running appear on buttons on the taskbar. To switch to a new application, click its button. You can also press Alt+Tab to cycle through all the open applications.

Part II

Setting Up and Editing a Document

In Part II, you'll find instructions for editing and doing the tasks that take up most of your word processing time. Among other things, Part II explains how to create, open, and close files. It tells you how to move around in documents, cut and copy text, and hyphenate and fix spelling errors.

My Word, there are a lot of good things in Part II.

In this part...

- ✔ Deleting, selecting, cutting, copying, and pasting text
- ✔ Finding and correcting spelling errors
- ✔ Opening and closing a document
- ✔ Exiting Word 95
- ✔ Saving a document
- ✔ Working with headers, footers, and page numbers
- ✔ Working with more than one document at once
- ✔ Zooming in and out on a document

Breaking a Line

You can break a line in the middle, before it reaches the right margin, without starting a new paragraph or pressing Enter. To do that, press Shift+Enter.

By pressing Shift+Enter, you can fix problems in the way Word breaks lines, and you can also break a line without starting a new paragraph. When words are squeezed into narrow columns, it often pays to break lines to remove ugly white spaces.

This figure shows two identical paragraphs in a column. To make the lines break better, I pressed Shift+Enter before the word *in* in the first line of the second paragraph. I did it again in the second-to-last line before the word *the*.

> "A computer in every home and a chicken in every pot is our goal," stated Ronald T. Darghassen, President and CEO of the NewTechnics Corporation International at the annual shareholders meeting last week.
>
> "A computer in every home and a chicken in every pot is our goal," stated Ronald T. Darghassen, President and CEO of the NewTechnics Corporation International at the annual shareholders meeting last week.

 Line breaks are marked with the ↵ symbol. To erase line breaks, click the Show/Hide ¶ button to see these symbols and backspace over them.

Breaking a Page

Word gives you another page so you can keep going when you fill up one page. But what if you're impatient and want to start a new page right away? Whatever you do, *don't* press Enter over and over until you fill up the page. Instead, create a page break by doing either of the following:

✦ Press Ctrl+Enter.

✦ Choose Insert⇨Break, click Page Break, and then click OK.

To delete a page break, backspace or delete over it. You know when you've inserted a page break yourself because you see the words Page Break and a dotted line instead of the dotted line at the end of the page.

TIP

If you have two paragraphs or a paragraph and graphic that you want to keep on the same page, or if you want a paragraph to stay on one page and not break across two pages:

1. Choose Format⇨Paragraph.

2. Click the Text Flow tab.

3. Choose Keep Lines Together to keep a paragraph intact, or choose Keep with Next to keep two paragraphs on the same page.

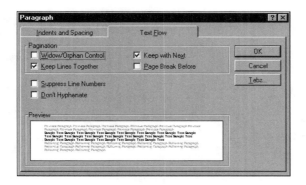

Changing the Look of the Screen

The Word 95 window is cluttered, to say the least, but you can do something about that with options on the View menu.

✦ Choose View⇨Full Screen if you want to get rid of everything except the text you're working on. When you choose Full Screen, everything gets stripped away — buttons, menus, scroll bars, and all. Only a single button called Full Screen remains. Click it or press Esc when you want the buttons, menus, and so on back.

✦ Choose View⇨Toolbars to remove toolbars. In the Toolbars dialog box, click to remove the check mark next to the toolbars you don't need. You can also right-click a toolbar and click the name of the toolbar you want to remove on the shortcut menu.

✦ Choose View⇨Ruler to get rid of the ruler.

Click to get Word 95 back

THE CHARLES P. SCHUMWAY CORPORATION

PROPOSAL AND
MARKETING PLAN

SCHUMWAY'S BEST OPPORTUNITY
FOR EAST ASIA EXPANSION

End of Section

PROPOSAL AND
MARKETING PLAN

SCHUMWAY'S BEST OPPORTUNITY FOR EAST ASIA EXPANSION

FINDING THE POWER TO DO OUR BEST!

Not since Colonel Perry docked his mighty fleet in Tokyo Bay have there been so many opportunities for American companies in Japan.

Finally, if you're adamant about ridding your screen of clutter, choose Tools⇨Options, click the View tab in the Options dialog box, and remove the *X*s from the scroll bar and status bar check boxes in the Window area (see the following figure).

Changing lowercase to UPPERCASE, UPPERCASE to lowercase

What do you do if you look at your screen and discover to your dismay that you entered characters IN THE WRONG CASE? It happens.

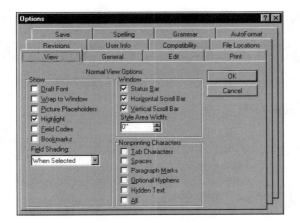

And sometimes Word does mysterious things to letters at the start of sentences and capital letters in the middle of words. What can you do about that?

You can fix uppercase and lowercase problems in two ways.

The fastest way is to select the text you entered incorrectly and press Shift+F3. Keep pressing Shift+F3 until the text looks right. Shift+F3 changes the characters to all lowercase, then to Initial Capitals, and then to ALL UPPERCASE.

The other way is to select the text, choose Format➪Change Case, and click an option in the Change Case dialog box:

+ **Sentence case:** Makes the text look like this.

+ **lowercase:** makes the text look like this.

+ **UPPERCASE:** MAKES THE TEXT LOOK LIKE THIS.

+ **Title Case:** Makes The Text Look Like This.

+ **tOGGLE cASE:** mAKES THE TEXT LOOK LIKE THIS, ALTHOUGH i'M NOT SURE WHY i WOULD CHOOSE THIS OPTION.

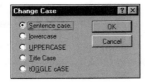

Microsoft Weird is very presumptuous about how it thinks capital letters should be used. You've probably noticed that already. You can't type a lowercase letter after a period. You can't enter a newfangled company name like QUestdata because Word refuses to let two capital letters in a row stand. You can't enter lowercase computer code at the start of a line without Word capitalizing the first letter. *See* "Correcting Typos on the Fly" in Part V if you want to change how Word 95 deals with capital letters.

Closing a Document

Choose File⇨Close to close a document when you're done working on it. If you try to close a document and you've made changes to it that you haven't saved yet, you see this dialog box:

Click Yes, unless you're abandoning the document because you want to start all over. In that case, click No.

TIP Click the Application Close button (the one with an X) in the upper-right corner of the screen to close a document and shut down Word 95 at the same time.

Copying, Moving, and Pasting Text

Word offers a number of different ways to copy and move text from one place to another. By one place to another, I mean from one part of a document to another, from one document to another document, and from one program to another program. Yes, you can even move and copy data between Windows-based programs.

Here's the conventional way to move or copy text:

1. Select the text to move or copy.

2. Do one of the following:

- **To move:** Choose Edit⇨Cut, click the Cut button, or press Ctrl+X.

- **To copy:** Choose Edit⇨Copy, click the Copy button, or press Ctrl+C.

3. Place the cursor where you want to move or copy the text.

4. Choose Edit⇨Paste, click the Paste button, or press Ctrl+V.

You can paste what is on the Clipboard into a document as many times as you want, or until you turn your computer off. If you like to decorate your correspondence with smiling faces, you can copy a smiley-face image to the Clipboard and keep pasting it in 'til the cows come home.

A fast way to cut, copy, and paste is to select the text, right-click it, and choose Cut or Copy from the shortcut menu. Then move the cursor where you want to paste the text, right-click, and choose Paste.

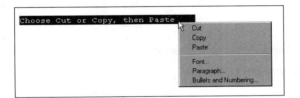

A second, slightly speedier way to move or copy text is to use the drag-and-drop method:

1. Select the text you want to copy or move.

2. Slide the mouse over the selected text until the cursor changes into an arrow.

3. Copy or move the text:

• **To move:** Drag the text to a new location.

• **To copy:** Hold down the Ctrl key while you drag the text elsewhere.

4. Let up on the mouse button.

One neat thing about dragging and dropping is that you can copy or move text without disturbing what's on the Clipboard. Text isn't copied to the Clipboard when you drag and drop.

When you move part of a sentence by dragging and dropping it, what to do with the blank spaces on the sides of the text chunk you're moving can be problematic. To help with that, Word has a thing called *Smart Cut and Paste*. It is supposed to take care of the blank space problem, but sometimes it proves a bother. If it seems bother-some to you (it does to me), you can turn off Smart Cut and Paste. Choose Tools⇨Options, go to the Edit tab, and remove the check mark next to the Use Smart Cut and Paste box.

Dashes

Amateurs make the hyphen do the work of the em dash and en dash. An *em dash* looks like a hyphen but is wider — it's as wide as the letter *m*. The last sentence has an em dash in it. Did you notice? If the sentence had a hyphen, it would look either like this, ". . . is wider-it's as wide as . . . ," or like this, ". . . is wider - it's as wide as . . ." That's the mark of an amateur.

An *en dash* is the width of the letter *n*. En dashes are used to show inclusive numbers or time periods, like so: pp. 45–50, Aug.–Sept. 1996, Exodus 16:11–16:18.

To place em or en dashes in your documents and impress your local typesetter or editor, not to mention your readers:

1. Choose Insert⇨Symbol.

2. Click the Special Characters tab in the Symbol dialog box.

3. Choose Em Dash or En Dash.

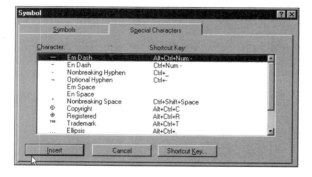

 Word may already be substituting your double hyphens for em dashes as part of its AutoCorrect mechanism. *See* "Correcting Typos on the Fly" in Part V.

Deleting Text

To delete a bunch of text at once, select the text you want to delete and press Delete or choose Edit⇨Clear.

See also "Undoing a Mistake" later in this part if you delete text and realize to your horror and dismay that you shouldn't have done that.

Exiting Word 95

When it's time to say good-bye to Word 95, save and close all your documents. Then do one of the following:

✦ Choose File⇨Exit.

✦ Click the Close button on the application window.

✦ Press Alt+F4.

If perchance you forgot to save and close a document, you'll see the `Do you want to save changes?` dialog box. Click Yes.

Finding and Replacing Text and Formats

The Edit⇨Replace command is a very powerful one indeed. If you were writing a Russian novel and you decided on page 816 to change the main character's last name from Oblonsky to Oblomov, you could do it on all 816 pages with the Edit⇨Replace command in about a half a minute.

But here's the drawback: You never quite know what this command will do. Newspaper editors tell a story about a newspaper that made it a policy to use the word *African-American* instead of *black*. A sleepy editor made the change with the Edit⇨Replace command and didn't review it. Next day, a lead story on the business page read, "After years of running in the red, U.S. Steel has paid all its debts, and now the corporation is running well in the African-American, according to company officials."

To replace words, phrases, or formats:

1. Choose Edit⇨Replace or press Ctrl+H.

2. Fill in the Find What box just as you would if you were searching for text or formats (see the "Finding Text and More" entry in this part to find out how).

3. In the Replace With box, enter the text that will replace what is in the Find What box. If you're replacing a format, enter the format.

4. Either replace everything at once or replace one thing at a time:

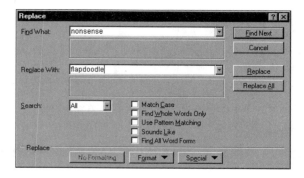

- Click Replace All to make all replacements in an instant.

- Click Find Next and then either click Replace to make the replacement or Find Next to bypass it.

Word tells you when you're finished.

The sleepy newspaper editor I told you about clicked the Replace All button. Only do that if you're very confident and know exactly what you're doing. In fact, you should click the Find Next button a few times to make sure that your Find What choices are really uncovering what you want to replace before you actually use the Edit⇨Replace command and "replace all." The Find dialog box has a button called Replace to help you with that.

Always save your document before you use the find and replace feature. Then, if you replace text that you shouldn't have replaced, you can close your document without saving it, open your document again, and get your original document back.

Finding the Right Word with the Thesaurus

If you can't seem to find the right word, you can always give the Thesaurus a shot. To find synonyms (words that have the same or a similar meaning) for a word in your document:

1. Place the cursor in the word.

2. Choose Tools⇨Thesaurus or press Shift+F7.

3. Begin your quest for the right word.

4. When you've found it and it appears in the Replace with Synonym box, click Replace.

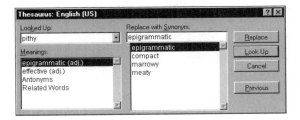

Finding the right words is nine-tenths of writing, so the Thesaurus dialog box tries to make it easier by offering these amenities:

+ **Loo_k_ed Up:** A scroll box with all the words you've investigated in your quest. Click a word here to go back to one you've examined (or click the _P_revious button).

+ **_M_eanings:** Different ways the term can be used — as a verb or noun, for example. Click here to turn your search in a different direction. Sometimes there's even an Antonym selection. At worst, if you know the opposite of the word you want, you can look it up in the Thesaurus and find its antonym. You can also try choosing Related Words if you're desperate.

+ **Replace with _S_ynonym:** If the Thesaurus isn't being helpful, you can always type a word into this box and click the _L_ook Up button.

+ **_L_ook up:** Highlight a word in the Replace with _S_ynonym box scroll list and click the _L_ook Up button to investigate that word.

Finding Text and More

You can search for a word in a document, and even for fonts, special characters, and formats. Here's how:

1. Choose _E_dit⇨_F_ind or press Ctrl+F. The Find dialog box appears.

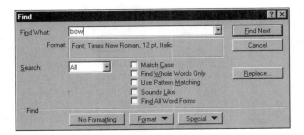

2. Type the word or phrase you're looking for in the Find What box.

3. In the Search drop-down menu, choose All, Up, or Down to search the whole document, search from the cursor position upward, or search from the cursor position downward.

4. Click check boxes to tell Word 95 how to conduct the search (these check boxes, and the Format and Special buttons, are described in a moment).

5. Click Find Next to start the search.

If the thing you're looking for can be found, Word highlights it in the document.

6. Click Find Next again to look for another instance of the word or phrase, or click outside the dialog box to make changes and then click Find Next, or click Cancel to quit searching.

You can get very selective about what to search for by choosing options and combinations of options in the Find dialog box:

✦ **Match Case:** Searches for words with uppercase and lowercase letters that exactly match those in the Find What box. With this box selected, a search for *bow* finds that word but not *Bow* or *BOW*.

✦ **Find Whole Words Only:** Normally, a search for *bow* yields *elbow, bowler, bow-wow,* and all other words with the letters *bow* in them. Click this option and you only get *bow*.

✦ **Use Pattern Matching:** Click here if you intend to use wildcards in searches. (Look under "Search Criteria" in the Word 95 Help Index to find out about them. You can also click the Special button to get wildcards.)

✦ **Sounds Like:** Looks for words that sound like the one in the Find What box. A search for *bow* with this option selected finds *beau*, for example.

✦ **Find All Word Forms:** Takes into account verb endings and plurals. With this option clicked, you get *bows, bowing,* and *bowed,* as well as *bow*.

To search for words, paragraphs, tab settings, and styles, among other things, that are formatted a certain way, click the Format button and choose an option from the menu. You see the familiar dialog box you used in the first place to format the text. In the Find dialog box shown in this book, I chose Font from the Format menu and filled in the Font dialog box in order to search for the word *bow* in Times New Roman, 12-point, italicized font.

Click the Special button to look for format characters, manual page breaks, and other unusual stuff.

That No Formatting button is there so you can clear all the formatting from the Find What box, and the Replace button is there in case you want to replace what you're searching for with something else. But to find out about that, you have to read "Finding and Replacing Text and Formats," also in this part.

Getting the Help You Need

 The Help button is the one in the upper-right corner next to the lightbulb. Click it, drag the question mark to whatever it is you need to know about, and click. With any luck, you'll get concise instructions for carrying out the thing you clicked. Click this button again when you're done reading the mini-Help screen. Here is the mini-Help screen you get when you click text to see how it is formatted:

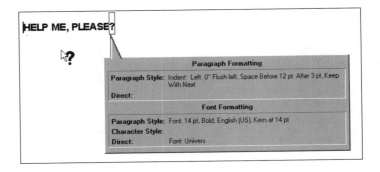

 The upper-right corners of dialog boxes also have Help buttons. Click a dialog box Help button and click the part of the dialog box you need help with to get a brief explanation of the thing you clicked.

If neither of these techniques works, press F1 or choose Help⇨Microsoft Word Help Topics. You'll see the Help Topics dialog box, which offers four different ways of getting help:

✦ **Contents:** A bunch of general topics. Click one, choose Open, and start reading if general topics are your cup of tea.

✦ **Index:** This is the most useful option. Click the Index tab and type a few letters that describe what puzzles you. The alphabetical list of index topics scrolls down to show you which topics are available. If a topic strikes your fancy, click it and choose Display. Either you'll get a second list of subtopics to choose from or you'll go straight to an informative instruction box or some other help feature.

✦ **Find:** With this option, you search for a word in the Help files. For example, if you need help with margins, type **margin.** A list of topics appears at the bottom of the dialog box. Click the topic you're interested in and click OK.

✦ **Answer Wizard:** On this tab, you can type an interrogative in the first box, click Search, hope for a sensible response in the second box, and if there is one, select it and click Display to see a help screen. (If you're fond of the Answer Wizard, you can get to it directly by choosing Help⇨Answer Wizard.)

The Help menu also has a special command for people who have switched over from the WordPerfect word-processing application and another to help you with The Microsoft Network, in case you're plugged in to that part of the Microsoft monopoly.

That last command on the Help menu, About Microsoft Word, is only of interest if your computer dies and you need technical help from Microsoft. I hope that doesn't happen, but if it does, choose this command and click the Tech Support button to find out how to contact Microsoft. Hmmm. I just realized something. You couldn't choose that command if your computer died, could you?

Grammar-Checking Your Document

Word's Grammar Checker is theoretically able to correct grammatical mistakes in a document. Personally, I think the thing is useless and don't recommend using it. And I'm not just saying that because I'm an editor and writer and I (supposedly) have mastered grammar. I just think that a machine can't tell what's good writing and what isn't. Period.

To use this instrument of highly dubious value:

1. Choose Tools⇨Grammar.

2. When the Robo-Grammarian stops on a sentence, you can either click Change to change the words or click Ignore to keep going.

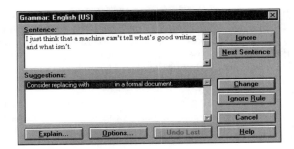

At the end of the grammar check, you get a bizarre screen that tells you, among other things, how many words you used on average in each sentence and what the grade level of your writing is (mine's sixth grade). This screen proves, once and for all, that writers at least will never be replaced by machines.

Hyphenating a Document

The first thing you should know about hyphenating a document is that you probably shouldn't do it. Text that hasn't been hyphenated is much easier to read — which is why the text in this book doesn't use many hyphens. It has a *ragged right margin,* to use typesetter lingo. Only hyphenate when text is trapped in columns or in other narrow places, when it is justified, or when you want a very formal-looking document.

You can hyphenate text as you enter it, but I think you should wait until you've written everything so you can concentrate on the words themselves. Then, when you're done with the writing, the best way to hyphenate is to let Word have a crack at it and then go back yourself and hyphenate the paragraphs that don't look right.

To hyphenate a document:

1. Choose Tools⇨Hyphenation.

2. Click Automatically Hyphenate Document to let Word do the job.

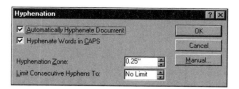

3. Click Hyphenate Words in CAPS to remove the check mark.
Never, ever hyphenate uppercase words if you can help it.

4. If the text isn't justified — that is, if it's "ragged right" — you
might play with the Hyphenation Zone setting (but I don't think
you should hyphenate ragged right text anyway). Words that fall
in the Zone are hyphenated, so a large zone means a less ragged
margin but more ugly hyphens, and a small zone means fewer
ugly hyphens but a more ragged right margin.

5. More than two consecutive hyphens in a row on the right margin
looks bad, so enter **2** in the Limit Consecutive Hyphens To box.

6. Click OK.

Word hyphenates your document.

Hyphenating a paragraph manually

With that done, see what kind of a job Word did. When you find a
paragraph that wasn't hyphenated well:

1. Select the paragraph.

2. Choose Tools➪Hyphenation.

3. Remove the check from the Automatically Hyphenate Document
box.

4. Click the Manual button. Word swings into Page Layout view (if
you're not already there) and displays a box with some hyphenation choices in it.

5. Click Yes or No to accept or reject Word's suggestion.

6. Keep accepting or rejecting Word's suggestions. At some point, a
box appears to tell you that Word has hyphenated the selection.
The box invites you to keep going.

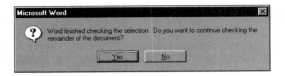

7. Click <u>N</u>o. Another box informs you that you're done.

8. Click OK and go on to the next paragraph that Word didn't hyphenate well.

Unhyphenating and other hyphenation tasks

Here is some more hyphenation esoterica:

+ To "unhyphenate" a document, choose <u>T</u>ools⇨<u>H</u>yphenation, remove the check from the <u>A</u>utomatically Hyphenate Document box, and click OK.

+ To keep a paragraph from being hyphenated, choose F<u>o</u>rmat⇨<u>P</u>aragraph, click the Text <u>F</u>low tab, and put a check mark in the <u>D</u>on't hyphenate box. If you can't hyphenate a paragraph, it is probably because this box was checked unintentionally.

+ If you want to hyphenate a single paragraph in the middle of a document — maybe because it's a long quotation or some other thing that needs to stand out — select it and hyphenate it manually by clicking the Manual button.

+ If there is a big gap in the right margin and a word is crying out to be hyphenated, move the cursor to where the hyphen should be and press Ctrl+hyphen. In this illustration, I pressed Ctrl+hyphen after *antidis* in the second paragraph.

```
On a "ragged right" margin, how
do you fix the big gaps that
sometimes appear when you use
long words like
"antidisestablishmentarianism?"

On a "ragged right" margin, how
do you fix the big gaps that
sometimes appear when you use
long words like "antidis-
establishmentarianism?"
```

Inserting a Whole File in a Document

One of the beautiful things about word processing is that you can recycle documents. Say you wrote an essay on the Scissor-Tailed Flycatcher that would fit very nicely in a broader report on North American birds. You can insert the Scissor-Tailed Flycatcher document in your report document:

1. Place the cursor where you want to insert the document.

2. Choose Insert➪File.

3. In the Insert File dialog box, find the file you want to insert.

4. Click OK.

Click to move up a directory

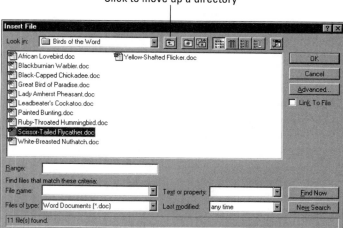

Moving Around in Documents

Documents have a habit of getting longer and longer, and as they do that it takes more effort to move around in them. Here are some shortcuts for moving the cursor in documents:

Key to Press	*Where It Takes You*
PgUp	Up the length of one screen
PgDn	Down the length of one screen
Ctrl+PgUp	To the top of the screen

Key to Press	Where It Takes You
Ctrl+PgDn	To the bottom of the screen
Ctrl+Home	To the top of the document
Ctrl+End	To the bottom of the document

You can also use the scroll bar to get around in documents. The *scroll bar* is the vertical stripe along the right side of the screen that resembles an elevator shaft. Here's how to move around with the scroll bar:

✦ To move through a document quickly, grab the elevator (called the *scroll box*) and drag it up or down.

✦ To move line by line up or down, click the up or down arrow at the top or bottom of the scroll bar.

✦ To move screen by screen, click anywhere on the scroll bar except on the arrows or the elevator.

By the way, there's another scroll bar on the bottom of the screen for moving from side to side.

A fast way to get from place to place is with the Edit⇨Go To command. Choose this command, enter a page number, and click Go To.

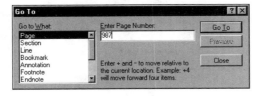

See also "Going Here, Going There in Documents" and "Bookmarks for Hopping Around" in Part V for more moving-around shortcuts.

Numbering the Pages

Word numbers the pages in a document automatically, which is great, but if your document has a title page and table of contents and you want to start numbering pages on the fifth page, or if your document has more than one section, page numbers can turn into a sticky business.

The first thing to ask yourself is whether you've included headers or footers in your document. If you have, go to "Putting Headers and Footers on Pages," also in this part. It explains how to put page numbers in a header or footer.

Meantime, use the Insert➪Page Numbers command to put plain old page numbers on the pages of a document:

1. Choose Insert➪Page Numbers to open the Page Numbers dialog box.

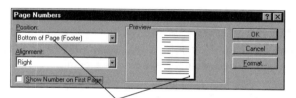

Where page numbers go

2. In the Position and Alignment boxes, choose where you want the page number to appear. The lovely Preview box on the right shows where your page number will go.

3. Click to remove the check mark from the Show Number on First Page box if you're working on a letter or other document that usually doesn't have a number on page 1.

4. Click OK.

If you want to get fancy, I should warn you that it's easier to do that in headers and footers than it is in the Page Numbers dialog box. Follow the first three steps in the preceding list and click the Format button. Then, in the Page Number Format dialog box:

✦ **Number Format:** Choose a new way to number the pages if you want to. (Notice the *i, ii, iii* choice. That's how the beginnings of books, this one included, are numbered.)

✦ **Include Chapter Number:** If you've used Word's Format➪ Heading Numbering command to title the chapters in your document, you can click this check box to include chapter numbers automatically. Pages in Chapter 1, for example, are numbered 1-1, 1-2, and so on.

✦ **Page Numbering:** This is the one that matters if you've divided your document into sections. Either start numbering the pages anew and enter a new page number to start at or else number pages where the preceding section left off.

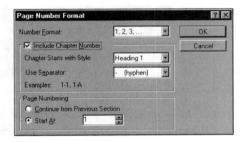

When you're done, click OK twice to number the pages and get back to your document.

To get rid of the page numbers if you don't like them:

1. Either choose View⇨Header and Footer or double-click the page number in Page view.

2. Click the Switch Between Header and Footer button, if necessary, to get to the footer.

3. Select the page number and press Delete.

Page number

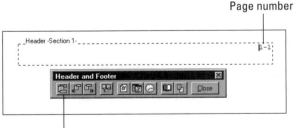

Click to go to footer or header

Suppose you have a title page and a table of contents in your document and want to start numbering pages on page 5. To do that, you have to divide your document into two sections and number only the second section. *See* "Dividing a Document into Sections" in Part III.

Opening an Existing Document

To open a document you've already created and named:

1. Choose File⇨Open, press Ctrl+O, or click the Open button.

Click to move up one level

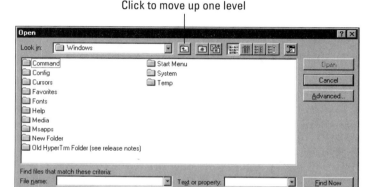

2. Find the folder where the file is. Where the file is depends on the folder you stored it in. To get to my Word 95 files, I have to click the Up One Level button, double-click the Microsoft Office folder, and double-click the Winword folder.

3. When you get to the folder the file is in, click the file to select it.

4. Click the Open button.

Opening a New Document

You can create a brand-new document in three different ways:

✦ Choose File⇨New.

✦ Press Ctrl+N.

✦ Click the New button.

If you opt for File⇨New, you see a dialog box with a bunch of stuff on it. For the moment, don't worry about letters, faxes, reports, memos, or templates. Just double-click the Blank Document icon or click OK to open a new document.

If you're opening a document you worked on recently, it might be on the <u>F</u>ile menu. Check it out. Open the <u>F</u>ile menu and see if the document you want to open is one of the four listed at the bottom of the menu. If it is, click its name or press its number (<u>1</u> through <u>4</u>).

Putting Headers and Footers on Pages

A *header* is a little description that appears along the top of a page so the reader knows what's what. Usually, headers include the page number and a title. A *footer* is the same thing as a header, except it appears along the bottom of the page, as befits its name.

To add a header or a footer:

1. Choose <u>V</u>iew⇨Header and Footer.

2. Type your header in the box or, if you want a footer, click the Switch between Header and Footer button and type your footer.

3. Click the <u>C</u>lose button.

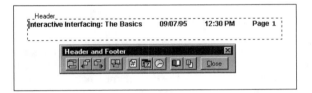

While you're typing away in the Header or Footer box, you can call on most of the commands on the toolbar and Formatting bar. You can change the text's font and font size, click an alignment button, or paste text from the Clipboard.

Button	What It Does
	Click this button on the Header/Footer toolbar to switch between the header and the footer.
	Click one of these buttons if you've divided your document in sections and you want to use a header or footer from the previous or next section.
	Click the date button, and the date you print your document will appear in the header. Click the time button to make the time you print your document appear in the header or footer.

(continued)

Button	What It Does
	Click this one to insert the page number. You can play around with this, too. For example, if you're in Chapter 2 (and the second section of your document), you can enter **Page 2-** and then click the Page button. You'd get `Page 2-1`, for example, in the header or footer on the first page of Chapter 2.
	Click this one if you're printing on both sides of the paper and want different headers on the left and right side of the page spread.
	Click this button to see the text on the page and get an idea of what the header or footer looks like in relation to the text.

Removing headers and footers is as easy as falling off a turnip truck:

1. Click View⇨Header and Footer or click the header or footer in Page Layout view.

2. Select the header or footer.

3. Press Delete.

Saving a Document for the First Time

After you open a new document and work on it, you need to save it. As part of saving a document for the first time, Word opens a dialog box and invites you to give the document a name. So the first time you save, you do two things at once — you save your work and name your document.

To save a document for the first time:

 1. Choose File⇨Save, press Ctrl+S, or click the Save button.

Up One Level button

Save As

Save in: Birds of the Word

African Lovebird.doc	Ruby-Throated Hummingbird.doc
Blackburnian Warbler.doc	Scissor-Tailed Flycather.doc
Black-Capped Chickadee.doc	White-Breasted Nuthatch.doc
Great Bird of Paradise.doc	
Lady Amherst Pheasant.doc	
Leadbeater.doc	
Leadbeater's Cockatoo.doc	
Painted Bunting.doc	

Save
Cancel
Options...

File name: Yellow-Bellied Sap Sucker.doc

Save as type: Word Document (*.doc)

2. Find and select the folder that you want to save the file in. To do that, you might have to click the Up One Level button and double-click folders in the main box until you arrive at the right folder.

3. Word 95 suggests a name in the File <u>n</u>ame box (the name comes from the first few words in the document). If that name isn't suitable, enter another. Be sure to enter one you will remember later.

4. If you're not saving a Word 95 document, click the Save as <u>t</u>ype drop-down list and click the type of document you're saving.

5. Click the <u>S</u>ave button.

Document names can be 255 characters long and can include all characters and numbers except these: / ? : * " < > |. They can even include spaces.

Keep the *.doc* ending on all Word documents. This ending, called a *file extension,* is how your computer knows that the document is a Word document and not a WordPerfect or Lotus 1-2-3 document, for example.

Instead of long document names, you might consider sticking with the old 8-character filenames that DOS uses. The problem with long names is that many of your friends and coworkers have applications that only accept 8-character filenames (11 characters if you count the 3-letter file extension). If you trade files with friends and your filenames are longer than 8 letters, your friends will have a hard time reading the long filenames.

Saving a Document under a New Name

If the name you gave to a document suddenly seems inappropriate or downright meaningless, or if you want to save the changes you make to a document in a new file, you can change the filename:

1. Choose <u>F</u>ile⇨Save <u>A</u>s.

2. Select a folder to save the newly named document in.

3. Give the document a new name in the <u>F</u>ile name text box.

4. If you're also changing the type of file this is, click the Save as <u>t</u>ype drop-down menu and choose the file type.

5. Click the <u>S</u>ave button.

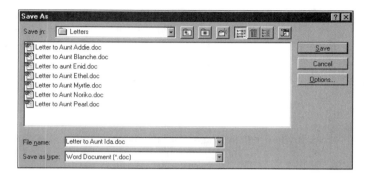

Now you have a second copy of the document, this one with a descriptive name. You might decide to delete the first copy.

The File➪Save As command has a side benefit: You can use it to make copies of files under different names. For example, suppose you're composing a letter to your Aunt Enid and it dawns on you that you could send the same letter, with minor modifications, to your Aunt Ida as well. Choose File➪Save As, save Letter to Aunt Enid.doc as Letter to Aunt Ida.doc, make sure that the salutations on both letters are correct, print the letters, and mail them. While I'm on the subject, you should write to your aunts. They've been asking about you.

Saving a Document You've Been Working On

It behooves you to save your documents from time to time as you work on them. (No, *behooves* is not computer jargon. The word just means that you should.) When you save a document, Word takes the work you've done since the last time you saved your document and stores the work safely on the hard disk.

You can save a document in three different ways:

+ Click the Save button.

+ Choose File➪Save.

+ Press Ctrl+S.

Save early and often. Make it a habit to click the Save button whenever you leave your desk, take a phone call, or let the cat out. If you don't save your work and there is a power outage or somebody trips over the computer's power cord, you lose all the work you did since the last time you saved your document.

Selecting Text in Speedy Ways

To move text or copy it from one place to another, you have to select it first. You can also erase great gobs of text merely by selecting them and pressing the Delete key. So it pays to know how to select text. Here are some shortcuts for doing it:

To Select This	Do This
A word	Double-click the word.
A line	Click in the left margin next to the line.
Some lines	Drag the mouse over the lines or drag the mouse down the left margin.
A paragraph	Double-click in the left margin next to the paragraph.
A mess of text	Click at the start of the text, hold down the Shift key, click at the end of the text, and let up on the Shift key.
A gob of text	Put the cursor where you want to start selecting, press F8 or hold down the Shift key, and press the arrow keys or drag the mouse.
Yet more text	If you select text and realize that you want to select yet more text, double-click EXT (it stands for Extend) on the status bar and start dragging the mouse or pressing arrow keys.
A document	Hold down the Ctrl key and click in the left margin, or triple-click in the left margin, or else choose Edit⇨Select All.

If you have a bunch of highlighted text on-screen and you want it to go away but it won't (because you pressed F8 or double-clicked EXT to select it), double-click EXT again.

When you roll the mouse over text to select it, Word selects text a word at a time. Some people find that annoying. If you're one of them, choose Tools⇨Options. On the Edit tab, click Automatic Word Selection to remove the check mark. Then Word selects text a character at a time.

Spacing Lines

To change the spacing between lines, select the lines whose spacing you want to change or simply put the cursor in a paragraph if you're changing the line spacing in a single paragraph. If you're just starting a document, you're ready to go.

Choose Format⇨Paragraph and pick an option in the Line Spacing drop-down list:

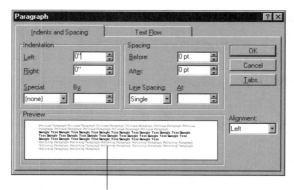

Watch this box!

◆ **Single, 1.5 Lines, Double:** These three options are quite up front about what they do.

◆ **At least:** Choose this one if you want Word to adjust for tall symbols or other unusual text. Word will adjust the lines but make sure there is, at minimum, the number of points you enter in the At box.

◆ **Exactly:** Choose this one and enter a number in the At box if you want a certain amount of space between lines and you can't get that amount with the Single, 1.5 Lines, or Double option.

◆ **Multiple:** Choose this one and put something in the At box to get triple-, quadruple-, quintuple-, or any other-spaced lines.

You can get a sneak preview of what your lines look like by glancing at the Preview box. Click OK when you've made your choice.

To quickly single-space text, select it and press Ctrl+1. To quickly double-space text, select it and press Ctrl+2.

You might notice the Before and After boxes in the Spacing area on the Indents and Spacing tab of the Paragraph dialog box. Use these boxes if you want blank space to be inserted automatically between paragraphs.

I must warn you that putting space between paragraphs is a sticky proposition. To Word's mind, a heading is also a paragraph, so if you put space between paragraphs, you may get strange blank spaces around your headings. And if you put space before *and* after para-graphs, you'll get twice the amount of space between paragraphs that you bargained for.

Spell-Checking Your Document

As you must have noticed by now, red, wiggly lines appear under words that are misspelled. Correct these words by right-clicking them and choosing an option from the shortcut menu. (If the red lines annoy you, or if you want to change how Word spell-checks documents, choose Tools➪Options and click the Spelling tab. Click to remove the check mark from Automatic Spell Checking.)

That's the one-at-a-time method for correcting misspelled words. You can also go the whole hog and spell-check an entire document or text selection by starting in one of these ways:

✦ Choose Tools➪Spelling.

✦ Press F7.

 ✦ Click the Spelling button.

The program stops on the first misspelled word. What you do next depends on whether the word in the Change To box is correct and how you want to handle the misspelled word. Here are your options:

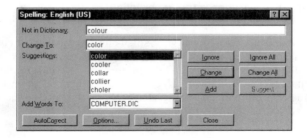

✦ **Change To:** This is the program's first choice for correcting the misspelling. You can type a word of your own in this box if you want to.

✦ **Ignore:** Ignores the misspelling but stops on it again if it appears later in the document.

+ **Ignore All:** Ignores the misspelling wherever it appears in the document. Not only that, it ignores it in all your other open documents as well.

+ **Change:** Click this button to insert the word in the Change To box in your document in place of the misspelled word.

+ **Delete:** The Delete button appears where the Change button is when the Spell-Checker finds two words in a row (*the the,* for example). Click Delete to remove the second word.

+ **Change All:** Changes not only this misspelling to the word in the Change To box, but all identical misspellings in the document.

+ **Add:** Adds the word in the Not in Dictionary box to the dictionary listed in the Add Words To scroll box so that the word is never called to question again. Click this button the first time that the spell-checker stops on your last name. By clicking this button, you add your last name to the spelling dictionary.

+ **Suggest:** Provides a list of more words to use in place of the misspelling.

+ **AutoCorrect:** Adds the suggested spelling correction to the list of words that are corrected automatically as you type them (*see* "Correcting Typos on the Fly" in Part V).

+ **Undo Last:** Goes back to the last misspelling you corrected and gives you a chance to repent and try again.

Suppose you have a bunch of computer code or Esperanto that you would like the spell-checker to skip and not waste time on. To keep the spell-checker from working on text, select the text, choose Tools⇨Language, choose the [no proofing] option at the top of the scroll box and click OK.

You probably shouldn't trust your smell-checker, because it can't catch all misspelled words. If you mean to type *middle* but type *fiddle* instead, the spell-checker won't catch the error, because fiddle is a legitimate word. The moral is this: If you're working on an important document, proofread it carefully. Don't rely on the spell-checker to catch all your smelling errors.

Symbols and Special Characters

You can decorate your documents with all kinds of symbols and special characters. Here's how:

1. Choose Insert⇨Symbol.

2. Click in the Font box to choose a symbol set.

3. Click a symbol. You see a bigger picture of it on-screen.

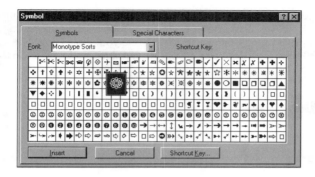

4. Click Insert.

The symbol you choose is placed in your document, but the Insert dialog box stays open so that you can select another symbol. Click Cancel or press Esc when you're done.

You can also choose special characters and unusual punctuation from the Special Characters tab of the Symbol dialog box.

Tall symbols require a lot of vertical space and sometimes affect the amount of space between lines. After you insert a symbol, switch to Page Layout view to see if it messed up the leading (*leading* is the space between lines). If it did, select the symbol and reduce its point size by using the Font Size drop-down list.

Undoing a Mistake

Fortunately for you, all is not lost if you make a big blunder in Word 95, because Word 95 has a thing called the Undo command.

This command "remembers" your last 99 editorial changes and puts them on the Undo drop-down menu. As long as you can identify an error on the list of 99, you can "undo" your mistake. There are two ways to undo:

❖ Choose Edit⇨Undo. This command changes names, depending on what you did last. Usually, it says Undo Typing, but if you move text, for example, it says Undo Move. Anyhow, select this command to undo your most recent action.

❖ Click the Undo button to undo your most recent change. If you made your error and went on to do something else before you caught it, click the down arrow next to the Undo button. You'll see a menu of your actions. Click the one you want to undo. However, if you do this, you also undo all the actions on the Undo menu that are above the one you're undoing. The same holds for the 99 actions on the scroll menu. If you undo the 98th on the list, you also undo the 97 before it.

What if you commit a monstrous error but can't correct it with the Undo command? You can try closing your document without saving the changes you made to it. As long as you didn't save your document after you made the error, the error won't be in your document when you open it again — but neither will the changes you want to keep.

Viewing Documents in Different Ways

Word offers the following ways of viewing a document:

+ **Normal view:** Choose View⇨Normal or click the Normal view button (in the lower-left corner of the screen) when you want to focus on the words. Normal view is best for writing first drafts and proofreading.

+ **Page Layout view:** Choose View⇨Page Layout or click the Page Layout View button to see the big picture. You can see graphics, headers, and footers in Page Layout view. Rulers appear on the window so you can pinpoint where everything is. At the bottom of the scroll bar, in the lower-right corner, you'll find an extra pair of scroll buttons. Click them to "page through" a document — that is, to move up or down a page at a time.

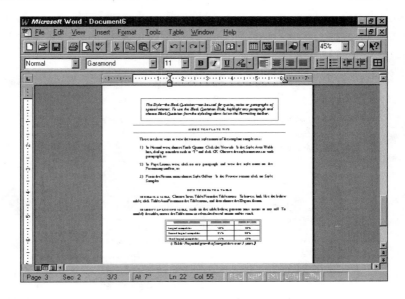

 ✦ **Outline view:** Choose View⇨Outline to see how your work is organized. In Outline view, you see only the headings and the first lines of paragraphs. To see a document in Outline view, you must have set up an outline. *See* "Outlines for Organizing Your Work" in Part V.

 To really hunker down and focus on the words, try changing to draft font. Choose Tools⇨Options. In the Options dialog box, click the View tab. Under Show, click the Draft Font check box. Draft font makes reading the words a lot easier and strips away all formats so you can concentrate on the text itself.

Working on Many Documents at Once

In Word, you can work on more than one document at the same time. You can even work in two different places in the same document (the "Working in Two Places in the Same Document" entry in this part tells how). All this magic is accomplished through the Window menu.

To see how the Window menu commands work, suppose for a moment that you're working on four poems — "Love," "Despair," "Hope," and "How I Yearn." It's the twilight hour and you're ready to compose, but you can't decide which poem to work on, so you open all four documents and wait for inspiration to strike.

When it does, select the Window menu and, depending on your mood, choose one of the four documents listed at the bottom of the menu. Alternately, you can put all four documents on-screen at once by choosing <u>W</u>indow⇨<u>A</u>rrange All. To go from one poem to the next, either click in a new window pane or press Ctrl+F6.

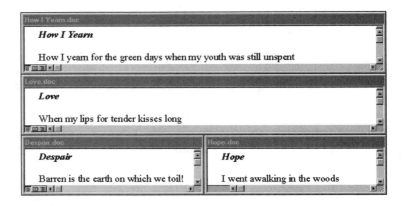

Suppose you're feeling sentimental and want to close the "Hope," "Despair," and "How I Yearn" window panes to concentrate on "Love." To do that, click the Minimize button of the window panes you don't want to see anymore. By doing so, you remove the other documents from the screen. Click the Restore button (the one in the middle with a square on it) to enlarge the window you want to work on to full-screen size.

Working in Two Places in the Same Document

You can open a window on two different places at once in a document. Here's one reason you might want to do this: You are writing a long report and want the introduction to support the conclusion, and you also want the conclusion to fulfill all promises made by the introduction. That's very, very difficult to do, but you can make it easier by opening the document to both places and writing the conclusion and introduction at the same time.

There are two ways to open the same document to two different places: by opening a second window or by splitting the screen.

Opening a second window

To open a second window on a document, choose <u>W</u>indow⇨<u>N</u>ew Window. Immediately, a second window opens up and you see the start of your document.

✦ If you open the <u>W</u>indow menu, you'll see that it now lists two versions of your document, *.doc:1* and *.doc:2*. Choose *.doc:1* to go back to where you were before.

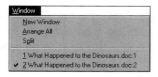

✦ You can move around in either window as you please. When you make changes in either window, you make them to the same document. Choose <u>F</u>ile⇨<u>S</u>ave in either window to save all the changes you made in both windows. The important thing to remember here is that you are working on a single document.

✦ When you want to close either window, just click its Close button. You go back to the other window, and only one version of your document appears on the <u>W</u>indow menu.

Splitting the screen

Splitting a window means to divide it into north and south halves. To do that, choose <u>W</u>indow⇨<u>S</u>plit. A gray line appears on-screen. Roll the mouse down until the gray line is where you want the split to be, and click. You'll get two screens split down the middle:

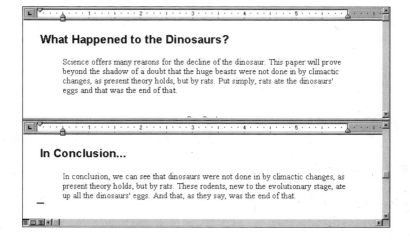

Now you have two windows and two sets of scroll bars along the right side of the screen.

✦ Use the scroll bars to move up or down on either side of the split, or press PgUp or PgDn, or press the arrow keys. Click the other side if you want to move the cursor there.

✦ When you tire of this schizophrenic arrangement, choose Window⇨Remove Split or drag the gray line to the top of the screen.

You can also split a screen by moving the cursor to the top of the scroll bar on the right. Move it just above the arrow. When it turns into a funny shape, click and drag the gray line down the screen. When you release the mouse button, you have a split screen.

Zooming In and Zooming Out

Eyes were not meant to stare at computer screens all day, which makes the Zoom command all the more valuable. Use this command to enlarge or shrink the text on your screen and preserve your eyes.

Enter a Zoom percentage here

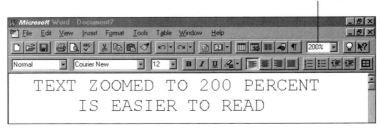

You can zoom in and out in two ways:

✦ Click the down arrow in the Zoom Control box on the toolbar (the box on the right side that shows a number followed by a percent sign) and choose a magnification percentage from the drop-down list.

✦ Click inside the Zoom Control box and type a percentage of your own.

Sometimes it pays to shrink the text way down to see how pages are laid out. For instance, after you lay out a table, shrink it way down to see how it looks from a bird's-eye view.

Part III

Formatting Documents and Text

Half the work in word processing is getting the text to look good on the page. "Appearances are everything," Oscar Wilde once remarked. The appearance of your documents should make as good an impression as their words, and that is what Part III is all about.

In this part...

- ✔ Changing the look of text
- ✔ Using the Style Painter, applying styles, and using other techniques to format text quickly
- ✔ Putting newspaper-style columns in documents
- ✔ Changing page margins, indentations, and tab settings
- ✔ Numbering lines and headings

Adding Bold, Italic, Underline, and Other Styles

It's easy to embellish text with **boldface,** *italics,* <u>underlines</u>, and other text styles. You can do it with the Format bar or by way of the Format⇨Font command. First, the Format bar:

✦ **Boldface:** Click the Bold button (or press Ctrl+B) and start typing. If you've already entered the text, select the text first and then click Bold or press Ctrl+B. Bold text is often used in headings.

✦ **Italics:** Click the Italic button (or press Ctrl+I). Select the text first if you've already entered it. Italics are used to show emphasis and also for foreign words such as *voilá, weltschmerz,* and *Que magnifico!*

✦ **Underline:** Click the Underline button (or press Ctrl+U). Select the text first and then click the button if you've already typed the text. You can also get double underlines with the Format⇨Font command.

The second way to get boldfaced, italicized, and underlined text is to choose Format⇨Font. When the Font dialog box appears, choose options from the Font Style scroll list.

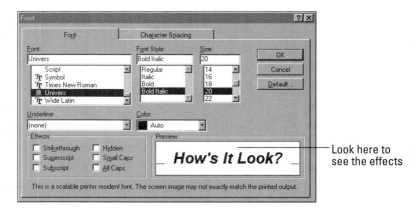

Look here to see the effects

The Font dialog box offers some other neat text styles:

✦ **Stri~~k~~ethrough:** I'm told that lawyers use ~~the strikethrough style~~ to show where text has been struck from legal contracts.

✦ **Superscript:** Used to mark footnotes in text, in math and scientific formulas ($E = MC^2$), and in ordinal numbers (1st, 2nd, 3rd).

✦ **Subscript:** Used in chemistry equations (H_2O).

✦ **Small Caps:** Used for time designations ("Columbus arrived in America on October 9 in AD 1492 at 11:30 A.M. eastern standard time"). Not all fonts can produce small capital letters.

✦ **Underline settings:** You can get dotted and double underlines as well as decide whether to underline the spaces between words.

It's easy to overdo it with text styles. Use them sparingly. For example, Johnny's words in the following illustration come straight from the heart, but somehow I think the message will be lost on Jane.

> Dearest Jane,
> How my **heart aches!** Those words I said—*surely you know darling how little I meant them.* But all is <u>not lost</u>.
> **Not lost I say!** We can *begin anew*. *We can!*

Centering, Justifying, and Aligning Text

All you have to do to align text in a new way is select the text and either click an Alignment button on the Format bar or press a keyboard shortcut:

Button	Button Name	Keyboard Shortcut	What It Does
	Align Left	Ctrl+L	Lines up text along the left margin.
	Center	Ctrl+E	Centers text, leaving space on both sides.
	Align Right	Ctrl+R	Lines up text along the right margin.
	Justify	Ctrl+J	Lines up text on both the left and right margins.

Text is aligned with respect to the left and right *margins,* not the left and right sides of the page. This illustration may give you a clearer idea of the alignment options:

Left-aligned text is used in most kinds of documents. It hugs the left margin. It is easiest to read. With left-aligned text, words break unevenly on the right margin.

Headings Are Often Center-Aligned

You don't see right-aligned text very often, but it has its uses. For example, the leftmost column on the first page of newsletters is often right-aligned. That's where "Notes from Our President" and articles of that kind go.

Justified text is good for formal documents and columns where lots of text has to be squeezed in a narrow space. You get uneven spaces between words with justified text. I think justified text should be hyphenated to keep those uneven spaces to a minimum.

You can also get alignment options from the Paragraph dialog box. Choose Format⇨Paragraph. The Alignment options are on an obscure drop-down menu in the lower-right corner of the dialog box.

Changing the Font of Text

Font is the catchall name for type style and type size. When you change fonts, you choose another style of type or change the size of the letters. Word 95 offers a whole bunch of different fonts. You can see their names by clicking the down arrow next to the Font menu and scrolling down the list.

To change the font:

1. Select the text.

2. Click the down arrow on the Font menu.

3. Scroll down the list, if necessary.

4. Click a font name.

Word 95 puts all the fonts you've used so far in the document at the top of the Font menu to make it easier for you to find them.

To change the size of letters:

1. Select the letters.

2. Click the down arrow on the Font Size menu.

3. Scroll down the list if you want a large font.

4. Click a point size — 8, 12, 36, 48, and so on.

You can also change font sizes quickly by selecting the text and pressing Ctrl+Shift+< or Chtrl+Shift+>.

Type is measured in *points*. The larger the point size, the larger the letters. Business and love letters usually use 10- or 12-point type. For headings, choose a larger point size. In this book, first-level main headings are 18 points high and are set in the Cascade Script font. The text you are reading is Cheltenham 9-point font.

You can also change fonts by choosing Format⊏⊃Font and making selections in the Font dialog box.

When you open a brand-new document and start typing, does the text appear in your favorite font? If it doesn't, you can make the font you use most often the default font:

1. Choose Format⊏⊃Font.

2. Choose the font in the dialog box.

3. Click the Default button.

4. Click Yes when Word 95 asks you if this font really should be the default font.

Creating Numbered and Bulleted Lists

Numbered lists are invaluable in manuals and books like this one that present a lot of step-by-step procedures. Use bulleted lists when you want to present alternatives to the reader. In this entry of the book, for example, there are two bulleted lists. A *bullet* is a black filled-in circle or other character.

For some reason, Microsoft Weird tries to format numbered lists for you. You type the first entry in the list, press Enter, type the second entry, and press Enter. A 3 appears. How do you make the list end at 2? Simple. You right-click the line where the 3 is and choose Stop Numbering from the shortcut menu:

You can prevent Word from formatting your numbered and bulleted lists by following these steps:

1. Choose Tools⊏⊃Options.

2. Click the AutoFormat tab.

3. Remove the check marks from the Automatic <u>N</u>umbered Lists and Automatic <u>B</u>ulleted lists check boxes.

If you're happy with the way Word 95 formats numbered and bulleted lists, you can just use this shortcut menu to format them. Here's what these commands do:

✦ **Bullets and Numbering:** Opens the Bullets and Numbering dialog box so you can get at its options. This is the same dialog box you see when you choose the <u>F</u>ormat⇨Bullets and <u>N</u>umbering command, which I explain shortly.

✦ **Promote:** Promotes the entry in a multilevel list. For example, step 1a becomes step 2.

✦ **Demote:** Demotes the entry in a multilevel list. Step 2 becomes step 1a.

✦ **Skip Numbering:** Lets you insert a paragraph between two steps. For example, if you want to describe step 2 with a paragraph before you go on to step 3, click Skip Numbering, type the paragraph, and press Enter. You land on step 3.

✦ **Stop Numbering:** Ends the numbered or bulleted list.

The fastest, cleanest, and most honest way to create a numbered or bulleted list is to enter the text without any concern for numbers or bullets. Just press Enter at the end of each step or bulleted entry. When you're done, select the list and click either the Numbering or Bullets button on the Format bar.

If you're an individualist and want numbered and bulleted lists to work your own way, you have to choose <u>F</u>ormat⇨Bullets and <u>N</u>umbering and choose options from the Bullets and Numbering dialog box:

✦ **<u>N</u>umbered tab:** Click a choice and then click OK to choose a new numbering scheme.

✦ **M<u>u</u>ltilevel tab:** From here, you can choose complex numbering schemes with sublevels.

✦ **<u>B</u>ulleted tab:** Opt for diamond-shaped, star-shaped, or arrow-shaped bullets instead of the drab default black hole.

✦ **H<u>a</u>nging Indent:** If you haven't noticed, numbered and bulleted lists have hanging indents — the number or bullet is flush with the left margin and the text is indented. You can make the text and numbers align with the left margin by clicking this check box.

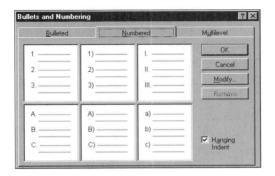

 TIP

The Start At box in the Modify Numbered List dialog box is very useful. If you write, say, three steps and then write several paragraphs of explanatory text and want to resume your numbered list at step 4, you can do so with this box. Choose Format⇔Bullets and Numbering, click the Modify button, and enter a **4** in the Start At box.

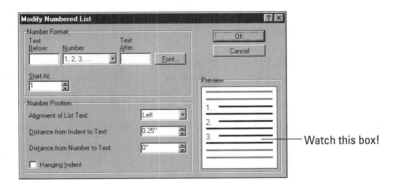

Watch this box!

Dividing a Document into Sections

Every document has one *section*. That's why "Sec 1" appears on the left side of the status bar at the bottom of the screen. When you want to change page numbering schemes, headers and footers, and margin sizes, you have to create a section break to start a new section. Word 95 creates one for you when you create columns or a table of contents.

To create a new section:

1. Click where you want to insert a section break.

2. Choose Insert⇨Break.

3. Tell Word 95 how to break the document. All four Section Breaks options create a new section, but they do so in different ways:

• **Next Page:** Inserts a page break as well as a section break so that the new section can start at the top of a new page (the next one). Select this option to start a new chapter, for example.

• **Continuous:** Inserts a section break in the middle of a page. Select this option, for example, if you want to change a header but don't want to insert a page break to do it.

• **Even Page:** Starts the new section on the next even page. This option is good for two-sided documents where the headers on the left- and right-hand pages are different.

• **Odd Page:** Starts the new section on the next odd page. You might choose this option if you have a book in which chapters start on odd pages (by convention, that's where they start).

4. Click OK.

You can tell where a section ends because `End of Section` and a double dotted line appear on-screen. To delete a section break, backspace over it.

Dropping In a Drop Cap

A *drop cap* is a large capital letter that "drops" into the text. Drop caps appear at the start of chapters in antiquated books, but you can find other uses for them. Here, a drop cap marks the A side of a list of songs on a homemade reggae tape.

A Bob Marley & the Wailers-Lively Up Yourself (1970) ✹Toots & the Maytals-Koo Koo (1968)✹Gregory Issacs-Slavemaster (1971)✹Junior Mervin-Police and Thieves (1973)✹Lynton Kwesi Johnson-England Is a Bitch (1978)✹Lee Perry & the Upsetters-Stop the War in Babylon (1969)✹Militant Dread-Children of the Most High (1974)✹ Charlie Goetchius Dread-Them na Downpress Di Union (1982)

To create a drop cap:

1. Type the letter you want to "drop." Don't worry about the font of this letter for now. Don't select the letter, either — just type it.

2. Choose Format⇨Drop Cap.

3. In the Drop Cap dialog box, choose which kind of drop cap you want by clicking a box. The None setting is for removing a drop cap.

4. Choose a font from the Font drop-down list. You should choose one that's different from the text in the paragraph. You can come back to this dialog box and get a different font later, if you wish.

5. Choose how many text lines the letter should "drop on."

6. Keep the 0 setting in the Distance from Text box unless you're dropping an *I, 0, 1,* or other skinny letter or number.

7. Click OK.

If you're not in Page Layout view, a dialog box asks whether you want to go there. Click Yes. You'll see your drop cap in all its glory.

The drop cap appears in a box or *text frame.* To change the size of the drop cap, you can tug and pull at the sides of the box (by dragging the handles with the mouse). However, you're better off choosing Format⇨Drop Cap again and playing with the settings in the Drop Cap dialog box.

Choose the None setting to remove a drop cap.

Formatting a Document

Word 95 offers a bunch of tools for formatting documents, some of them very complex. This section describes them.

You should double-check the words before you start formatting a document. It's easier to find mistakes and correct errors in raw text than it is to find and correct them in text that has been gussied up with different fonts and point sizes.

Fast formatting with the Format Painter

The fastest way to format a document is with the Format Painter. You can use this tool to make sure that the headings, lists, text paragraphs, and whatnot in your document are consistent with one another.

To use the Format Painter:

1. Click the text whose formatting you want to apply throughout your document. For example, if your document is a report with first-, second-, and third-level heads, format a first-level head so that it looks just right and click it.

2. Double-click the Format Painter. The mouse pointer changes into a paint roller icon.

3. Find the text you want to copy the format to, click the mouse button, and roll the mouse pointer over it as though you were selecting it. When you're done, the text takes on the new format.

4. Keep going. Find every place in your document that you can copy this format to and baste it with the Format Painter. You can click the scroll bar and use keyboard commands to move through your document.

5. Do the same for all the other formats you need to copy.

6. Click the Format Painter button when you're done.

Using styles for consistent formatting

If you have a little more time on your hands, and if you really want the headings, paragraphs, lists, and whatnot in your document to be consistent, use Word 95's style feature. The really neat thing about styles is that if you decide that a given style doesn't look right after you format a document, you can change it and have Word 95 instantly modify all paragraphs in your document to which you've assigned the given style.

Every document has five default styles to start with. You can see them by pulling down the Style menu on the Format bar:

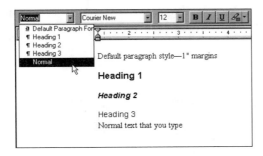

If these five do the job for you, you're all set. But chances are that you would like headings to appear in different fonts, and perhaps your document includes paragraphs that are indented in unusual ways, or five or six levels of headings, or numbered lists that you've formatted in exotic ways — whatever. You can add these styles to the Style menu. Then, when you want to format a paragraph, all you have to do is select a style from the menu.

Creating a new style

You can create new styles and add them to the Style menu in two ways: with the Format⇨Style command and directly from the screen. First, the directly-from-the-screen method:

1. Click a paragraph that is formatted in the style that you want to add to the menu. Remember, a heading is also a paragraph as far as Word 95 is concerned, so if you're creating a style for a heading, click the heading.

2. Click in the Style menu box and type a name for the style. Choose a meaningful name that you will remember.

3. Press Enter.

You can create a new style from scratch with the Format⇨Style command. It's a bit slower, but you get a few amenities that you don't get with the straight-from-the-screen method.

1. Choose Format⇨Style.

2. Click the New button.

3. Fill in the New Style dialog box. As you do so, keep your eyes on the Preview box. It shows you what your new style will look like in a document.

Watch this box!

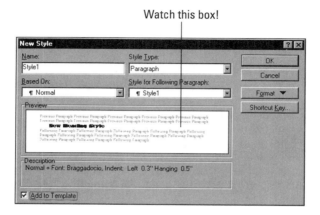

- **Name:** Enter a name for the style. The name you enter appears on the Style menu.

- **Style Type:** Click the down arrow and choose Character if you're creating a style for characters rather than paragraphs. If you often use an exotic font, you can create a style for it and simply click the style name on the Style menu instead of going to the trouble of formatting the characters in the document.

- **Based On:** If your new style is similar to one that is already on the menu, click here and choose the style to get a head start on creating the new one.

- **Style for Following Paragraph:** Choose a style from the drop-down list if the style you're creating is always followed by an existing style. For example, a new style called "Chapter Title" might always be followed by a style called "Chapter Intro Paragraph." If that were the case, you would choose "Chapter Intro Paragraph" from this drop-down list.

- **Format:** This is the important one. Click the button and make a formatting choice. Word 95 takes you to dialog boxes so that you can create the style.

- **Shortcut Key:** Opens a dialog box so that you can apply the new style simply by pressing a shortcut key combination.

- **Add to Template:** Adds the style to the document's template.

4. Click OK to close the New Style dialog box.

5. Click <u>A</u>pply to format the paragraph.

Applying a style to text and paragraphs

After you create a style and add it to the Style menu, applying it is as easy as pie:

1. Click the paragraph you want to apply the style to. If you're applying a character style, select the letters whose formatting you want to change.

2. Click the down arrow on the Style menu to see the list of styles.

3. Click a style name.

You can also take the long way around by choosing F<u>o</u>rmat⇨<u>S</u>tyle, choosing a style from the <u>S</u>tyles list in the Style dialog box, and clicking <u>A</u>pply. Take the long way around if you're not sure what a style is. You can see it in the Paragraph Preview and Character Preview boxes before you apply it.

Look in these boxes!

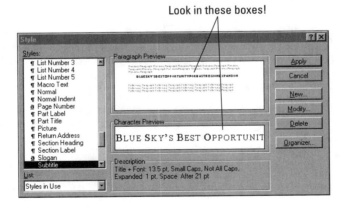

Changing a style throughout a document

What if you decide at the end of an 80-page document that all 35 introductory paragraphs to which you've assigned the "Intro Para" style look funny? You can change them instantaneously. You can reformat the paragraph so that it looks right and have Word 95 also change the other paragraphs in the document to which you have assigned the same style. Here's how:

1. Go to any paragraph to which you've assigned the style you want to change.

2. Reformat the paragraph.

3. Click the first name in the Style menu — it should be the name of the style whose formats you're changing.

4. Click anywhere on-screen. The Reapply Style dialog box appears:

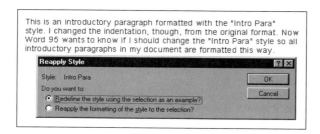

5. Click the Redefine the style using the selection as an example? check box.

6. Click OK.

I usually see the Reapply Style dialog box when I'm hurriedly formatting a document and accidentally click the wrong style on the Style menu. When you're formatting in a hurry, the Reapply Style dialog box has a way of popping on-screen when you least expect it. Just click Cancel when that happens.

If you've devised a tortuously complicated style and want to change it, use the Modify Style dialog box. Choose Format⇨Style and click the Modify button in the Style dialog box. If the Modify Style dialog box looks familiar, that's because it is identical to the New Style dialog box you used to create the style in the first place. Change the settings, click OK, and click Apply to apply the new style throughout your document.

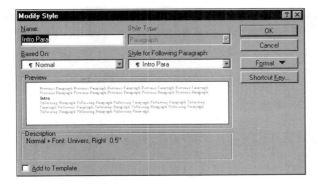

Using styles from the Style Gallery

The rogues' gallery of product designers who work at Microsoft knew that you would need a lot of different styles to do your work, so they invented the Style Gallery, a collection of templates that you can use to format documents.

The templates in the Style Gallery are the same ones you see when you choose File⇨New to open a new document.

A *template* is an assortment of different styles. New documents have the Normal template, the one that offers only five styles — Default Paragraph, Heading 1, Heading 2, and so on. Templates in the Style Gallery offer far more styles than that. And these styles were invented by pros, so they look good for the most part.

To add styles from a template in the Style Gallery to the styles you're already using in your document:

1. Choose Format⇨Style Gallery.

2. From the Template list, choose a template that most nearly describes what your document is and see what happens to it in the wide-screen Preview of box.

3. Click the Example check box to get a better look at what the template you chose has to offer.

4. Click the Style Samples check box. The Preview of box shows the names of the styles in the template and how the styles are formatted.

5. After you play around with Style Gallery for a while and find a template that suits you, click OK.

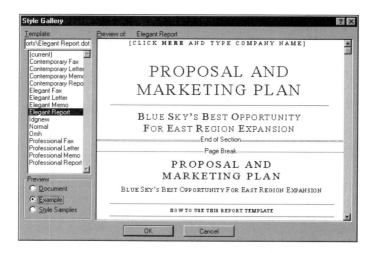

Formatting a document automatically

You can perform radical cosmetic surgery on documents with the Format⇨AutoFormat command. This command compares the styles on the document template with the text in the document and tries to match the right style with the right paragraph. When it's done, you get a chance to review the changes made to the document one at a time and accept or reject them.

Here's how it works:

1. Choose Format⇨AutoFormat. A dialog box tells you that your document is about to be formatted automatically. Click the Options button if you want to be specific about how your document is "AutoFormatted."

2. Click OK in the dialog box. Another dialog box tells you that the formatting has been done.

3. Glance at your document to see what AutoFormat has wrought and click one of the buttons:

- **Accept:** Accepts all the changes made to your document.

- **Reject All:** Rejects all the changes.

- **Review Changes:** Lets you go through the document one change at a time and accept or reject each change.

- **Style Gallery:** Takes you to the Style Gallery dialog box, where you can choose a new template. If you opt for this one, your document will be "AutoFormatted" a second time with the new template.

If you choose Accept or Reject All, you're done. Otherwise, the Review AutoFormat Changes dialog box appears so that you can review the changes one at a time. Where changes were made, blue revision marks appear on your document. To accept or reject the revisions, go on to step 4.

4. Click Find to see the first revision mark. You can see it on-screen, and the dialog box tells you what it is.

5. Click Reject to reverse it or Find to accept it and go on to the next revision.

6. Keep doing this until, gratefully, you reach the end of the document.

7. Click Cancel to tell Word 95 that you don't want to go to the top of the document and run the gauntlet again.

8. Click Accept in the final dialog box.

Indenting Paragraphs and First Lines

An *indent* is the distance between a margin and the text. Word 95 offers a handful of different ways to change the indentation of paragraphs.

The fastest way is to use the Increase Indent and Decrease Indent buttons on the Format bar to move the paragraph away from or toward the left margin:

1. Click in the paragraph whose indentation you want to change. If you want to change more than one paragraph, select them.

2. Click one of the buttons:

- **Increase Indent:** Indents the paragraph from the left margin by one tab stop (you can also press Ctrl+M).

- **Decrease Indent:** Moves the paragraph back toward the left margin by one tab stop (you can also press Ctrl+Shift+M).

You can also change indentations by using the ruler to "eyeball it." This technique requires some dexterity with the mouse, but it allows you to see precisely where paragraphs and the first lines of paragraphs are indented.

1. Select the paragraph or paragraphs whose indentation you want to change.

2. Slide the indent markers with the mouse:

- **First-line indent marker:** Drag the down-pointing arrow on the ruler to indent the first line of the paragraph only.

- **Left indent marker:** This one, on the bottom-left side of the ruler, comes in two parts. Drag the arrow that points up, but not the box underneath it, to move the left margin independently of the first-line indentation. To move the left indentation *and* the first-line indentation relative to the left margin, slide the box. Doing so moves everything on the left side of the ruler.

- **Right indent marker:** Drag this one to move the right side of the paragraph away from the right margin.

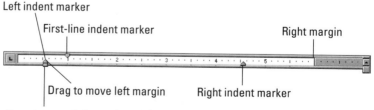

Left indent marker

First-line indent marker

Right margin

Drag to move left margin

Right indent marker

Drag to move left margin <u>and</u> first-line indent

You can create neat effects by dragging the first-line indent marker toward the margin to create a *hanging indent.* In the illustration you can see four hanging indents, two in the headings and two in the bulleted list (Word 95 puts hanging indents in bulleted lists automatically):

If you're not one for "eyeballing it," you can use the Format⇨Paragraph command to indent paragraphs:

1. Choose Format⇨Paragraph or double-click the Left or Right indent marker on the ruler.

2. Choose options in the Indentation area.

3. Click OK.

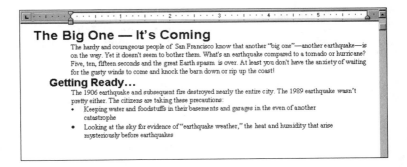

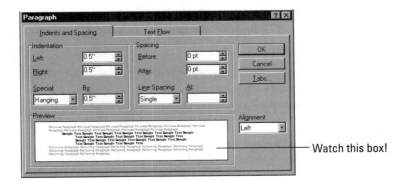

Watch this box!

The Indentation options are self-explanatory. As you experiment, watch the Preview box — it shows exactly what your choices will do to the paragraph. In the Special drop-down list, you can choose Hanging to create a hanging indent or First Line to indent the first line from the left margin. Enter a measurement in the By box to say how far you want these indents to travel. Did you notice that Alignment drop-down list in the lower-right corner? You can even align paragraphs from this dialog box.

Numbering the Headings in a Document

In scholarly papers and formal documents, the headings are some-times numbered so that cross-references and commentary can refer to them by number as well as by name. The Format⇨Heading Numbering command makes numbering the headings in a document very easy. The beauty of this command is that Word renumbers the headings automatically if you remove a heading or add a new one.

To use the Format⇨Heading Numbering command, you must have assigned Heading styles to your document. First-level heads are given top billing in the numbering scheme. Subheadings get lower billing.

To number the headings in a document:

1. Choose Format⇨Heading Numbering.

2. Click a box in the Heading Numbering dialog box. The top three boxes are different numbering schemes. The lower three boxes merely assign chapter numbers or appendix letters to all the Heading 1s in the document. Subheads are not numbered if you choose one of the lower three boxes.

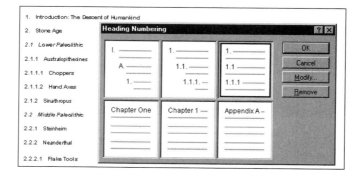

3. Click the Modify button if you want to devise your own number-ing scheme or put a word before all headings. You can even choose new fonts for headings. If you experiment, be sure to watch the Preview box to see what kind of damage you're doing. Click OK when you're done experimenting.

4. Click OK to close the Heading Numbering dialog box.

If you regret having numbered the headings in your document, either choose Heading Numbering from the Undo menu or open the Heading Numbering dialog box and click Remove.

Numbering the Lines in a Document

You can number lines very easily with Word 95. The numbers appear in the margin.

1. If you want to number the lines in one section only, place the cursor in that section. To number lines starting at one place, put the cursor where you want to start numbering. To number all the lines in the document, it doesn't matter where you place the cursor.

2. Choose File⇨Page Setup.

3. In the Page Layout dialog box, click the Layout tab.

4. Click the Line Numbers button.

5. In the Line Numbers dialog box, click the Add Line Numbering check box.

6. Choose options from the Line Numbers dialog box:

- **Start At:** Enter the number to begin counting with if you want to begin with a number other than 1.

- **From Text:** Determines how far the numbers are from the text. The larger the number you enter, the closer the numbers appear to the left side of the page.

- **Count By:** All lines are numbered, but by choosing a number here you can make numbers appear at intervals. For example, entering **5** makes intervals of five (5, 10, 15, and so on) appear in the margin.

- **Numbering:** In legal contracts, the numbers begin anew on each page, but you can start numbering at each section or number all lines in the document consecutively.

7. Click OK.

8. Back on the Layout tab of the Page Setup dialog box, choose an Apply To option from the drop-down list. If you're numbering only a section, choose This Section. Otherwise, choose Whole

Document to number all the lines or This Point Forward to number lines starting at the cursor.

9. Click OK.

To remove line numbers, follow steps 1 through 5 of the preceding set of instructions, but this time remove the check mark from the Add Line Numbering check box. Then click OK and click OK again in the Page Setup dialog box.

Putting Newspaper-Style Columns in a Document

Columns look great in newsletters and similar documents. And you can pack a lot of words in columns. With columns, you can present more than one document on a single page so readers have a choice of what they read.

Before you put text in newspaper-style columns, write it. Take care of the spelling, grammar, and everything else because it is hard to make text changes to words after they've been arranged in columns.

There are two ways to create columns: with the Columns button on the toolbar and with the Format⇨Columns command. Format⇨Columns gives you considerably more leeway because the Columns button only lets you create columns of equal width. To use the Columns button:

1. Select the text.

2. Switch to Page Layout view by clicking the Page Layout View button or choosing View⇨Page Layout. You can see columns only in Page Layout view.

3. Click the Columns button on the toolbar. A menu drops down so that you can choose how many columns you want.

4. Click one, two, three, or four columns.

Very likely, your columns don't look so good. It's hard to get it right the first time. You can drag the column border bars on the ruler to widen or narrow the columns:

Column border bars

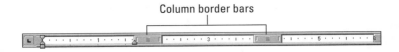

However, it's much easier to choose Format⇨Columns and play with options in the Columns dialog box. If you want to start all over, or if you want to start from the beginning with the Columns dialog box, here's how:

1. Select the text.

2. Switch to Page Layout view if you're not already there.

3. Choose Format⇨Columns.

4. Choose options from the Columns dialog box. As you do so, keep your eye on the Preview box in the lower-right corner.

Watch this box!

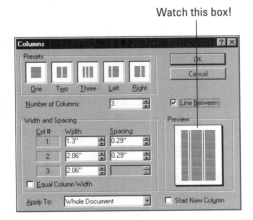

- **Presets:** Click a box to choose a preset number of columns. Notice that, in some of the boxes, the columns aren't of equal length. Choose One if you want to remove columns from a document.

- **Number of Columns:** If you want more than three columns, enter a number here.

- **Line Between:** Click this box to put lines between columns.

- **Col #:** If your document has more than three columns, a scroll bar appears to the left of the Col # boxes. Scroll to the column you want to work with.

- **Width:** If you click the Equal Column Width box to remove the check mark, you can make columns of unequal width. Change the width of each column by using the Width boxes.

- **Spacing:** Determines how much blank space appears between columns.

- **Equal Column Width:** Click this box to remove the check mark if you want columns of various widths.

- **Apply To:** Choose Selected Text unless you want to "columnize" the whole document, in which case you should choose Whole Document.

- **Start New Column:** This box is for putting empty space in a column, perhaps to insert a text frame or picture. Place the cursor where you want the empty space to begin, open the Columns dialog box, click this check box, and choose This Point Forward from the Apply To drop-down menu. Text below the cursor moves to the next column. (A faster way to do this is to press Ctrl+Shift+Enter where you want to break the column.)

5. Click OK.

TIP

After you do the initial layout, click the Zoom Control button and shrink the page to around 50 percent to get "the big picture" (another way to get the big picture is to choose File⇨Print Preview). Then start playing around with the column layout.

A DOG'S LIFE

The Newsletter for Pedigreed Pooches — and their Owners!

Notes from the Editor...

This season was a good one for the pedigreed community. Besides the Annual Fall Dog Show at the Midway County fairgrounds, several groups around the county staged smaller dog shows of their own. And each one, I'm happy to report, was a winner. Hats off especially go to the Northern New York Irish Setter Aristocrats, who put on a wonderful affair at the Crystal Palace last October 16. Lots of Fish Setters made new friends at the show, as did, of course, their owners. And lots of "matches made in heaven" were arranged at the show, too, or so I'm told by Mrs. Mervin Linksetter of Wyanneck and Mrs. Charles M. Tutterburg of Possborough. In the annals of dog breeding in America, surely this year will go down as one of the finest.

And on a final note: I would like to thank Mrs. Gloria Stevenson for her excellent work with basset hounds. Gloria, you have done much to improve the basset stock and when the real story of dog breeding is written, your name will surely have a place on the marquee, I warrant.

NYATT BREEDFEST BIG SUCCESS

Lots of "Matches Made in Heaven"

This year's Breedfest at Willoway Park was a runaway success. Many love matches were made, and both dogs and their owners came away satisfied not only with the way the event was organized, but by the excellent food. Unlike past Breedfests, which sometimes turned into bawdy affairs with the canines running amok on each other, this one was tastefully arranged.

Upon arrival, dog owners registered their pooches and were assigned breeding grounds at various locations in the park. There were no mishaps, this scribe is happy to report. I doubt if this year's Breedfest, unlike the poorly organized 1994 affair, will produce any mongrels or hybrids.

With the breeding done, owners and their charges settled down to a wonderful catered sit-down lunch featuring New York steak, kidney pie, and a sausage selection this scribe has not had the pleasure of relishing since a trip he took several years ago to Italy and Germany (but that's another story).

In short, it was a superb Breedfest, and an especially big "thank you" is owed to all the organizers in Nyatt.

You can do all this from the Columns dialog box and with the File⇨Page Set<u>u</u>p⇨<u>M</u>argins command.

If you decide to justify the columns, be sure to hyphenate them, too. It's not easy to get text in narrow columns to look good because so much empty space appears between words. To fix that, enter manual hyphens (press Ctrl+hyphen) and line breaks (press Shift+Enter) where necessary.

See also Part VI for information about including pictures and text boxes in columns.

Setting Up and Changing the Margins

Margins are the empty spaces between the text and the left, right, top, and bottom edges of a page. Headers and footers are printed in the top and bottom margins, respectively.

Don't confuse margins with indents. Text is indented from the margin, not from the edge of the page. If you want to change how far a paragraph is indented, use the ruler or the F<u>o</u>rmat⇨<u>P</u>aragraph command and change its indentation.

To change the margin settings:

1. Place the cursor where you want to change margins. You can change the margins in only one section at a time, so if your document has more than one section, place the cursor in the section for which you want to change margins.

2. Choose <u>F</u>ile⇨Page Set<u>u</u>p.

Watch this box!

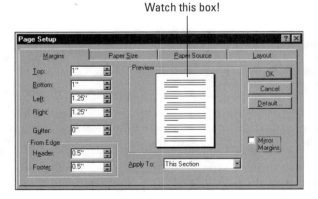

3. Choose the settings on the Margins tab and watch the Preview box to see what your choices do:

- **Top, Bottom, Left, Right:** Set the top, bottom, left, and right margins.

- **Gutter:** Allows extra space on the inside margin for documents that will be bound. Click the up arrow to see what binding looks like as it eats into the left side of the page and alters the left margin.

- **Header:** Makes the top margin bigger so you can fit two or three lines in headers.

- **Footer:** Makes the bottom margin higher for footers.

- **Apply To:** Choose Whole Document to apply your settings to the entire document, This Section to apply them to a section, or This Point Forward to change margins for the rest of a document. When you choose This Point Forward, Word 95 creates a new section.

- **Mirror Margins:** Makes room for the binding on pages that will be bound and on which text will be printed on both sides.

4. Click OK.

You can change the top and bottom margins with the horizontal ruler in Page Layout view. Simply drag the margin bar up or down.

If you don't care for Word 95's default margin settings, make your own in the Page Setup dialog box and click the Default button. Henceforth, new documents that you open will have *your* margin settings.

Working with the Ruler

The ruler along the top of the screen is there to help you change and identify margins, tab settings, and indents, as well as place graphics and text frames. (If you don't see it, choose View⇨Ruler.)

In Page Layout view, there is a similar ruler along the left side of the screen.

You can change the unit of measurement that is shown on the rulers. Choose Tools⇨Options, click the General tab, and choose Inches, Centimeters, Points, or Picas from the Measurement Units drop-down list. Here is what the horizontal ruler looks like with point measurements:

| L | 36 | 72 | 108 | 144 | 180 | 218 | 252 | 288 | 324 | 360 | 398 | 469 |

See also "Indenting Paragraphs and First Lines," "Setting Up and Changing the Margins," and "Working with Tabs" in this part to learn how to do those things with the rulers.

Working with Tabs

When you press the Tab key, you advance the text cursor by one tab stop. Tab stops are set at half-inch intervals on the ruler, but you can change that if you want to.

You can also change the type of tab. By default, tabs are left-aligned, which means that when you enter letters after you press the Tab key, the letters move toward the right in the same way that they move toward the right when text is left-aligned. However, Word 95 also offers right, center, and decimal tabs. This table shows how left, center, right, and decimal tabs work.

Left	Center	Right	Decimal
January	January	January	January
July	July	July	July
October	October	October	October
123	123	123	123
13,579.1	13,579.1	13,579.1	13,579.1
$45.95	$45.95	$45.95	$45.95

To change tabs or change where tabs appear on the ruler:

1. Click in the box on the left side of the ruler to get different tab settings. As you click, the symbols change, as shown:

Symbol	Tab Type
L	Left-aligned tab
⊥	Center-aligned tab
⅃	Right-aligned tab
⅃	Decimal tab

2. When you come to the symbol that represents the type of tab you want, click the ruler where you want to put a tab stop. You can click as many times as you want and enter more than one kind of tab.

Here is a ruler with all four kinds of tabs on it:

TIP

You can move tabs on the ruler simply by dragging them to new locations. Text that has been aligned with the tabs moves as well, if you select it first. To remove a tab, drag it off the ruler.

You can also make tab settings with the Tabs dialog box:

1. Place the cursor where you want your new tab settings to take effect. Or else select the text to which you want to apply your new tabs.

2. Choose Format⇨Tabs.

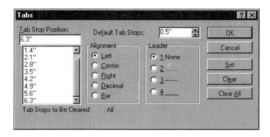

3. Enter a position for the first new tab in the Tab Stop Position box.

4. Choose an Alignment option. The Bar option places a vertical bar at the tab stop position. You can place numeric figures inside these bars, for example, to help line up numbers.

5. Choose a leader, if you want one. For example, if you choose 2, Word 95 places periods in the document whenever you press Tab at this setting. A *leader* is a series of identical characters. Leaders are often found in tables of contents — they are the periods between the table of contents entry and the page number it refers to.

6. Click the Set button.

7. Repeat steps 4 through 6 for the next tab setting and all other tab settings. If you change your mind about a setting, select it in the Tab Stop Position scroll box and click Clear. Click Clear All if you change your mind in a big way and want to start all over.

8. Click OK.

Printing Your Documents

What is a document until you print it? Not much. It's like an idea that hasn't been written down or communicated to anyone yet. A document isn't worth much until you run it through the printer and put it on paper so that other people can read it.

Part IV explains how to print documents in Word 95. It describes how to print labels and addresses on envelopes, print on sheets of paper other than the standard 8.5 x 11, and set up the pages for printing. This part also tells you what to do if you just can't get your documents to print.

In this part...

 ✔ **Seeing what you print before you print it**

 ✔ **Printing envelopes and address labels**

 ✔ **Printing on legal-size and other odd-shaped paper**

 ✔ **Telling Word 95 how to print a document**

 ✔ **Solving problems with the printer**

Previewing What You Print

 Before you print a document, do yourself a big favor by *previewing* it. That way, you can catch errors before you send them through the printer and waste 1, 2, 5, or 20 sheets of paper.

To preview a document:

1. Put the document you're about to print on-screen.

2. Choose File⇨Print Preview or click the Print Preview button on the toolbar. A panoramic picture of your document appears on the Preview screen:

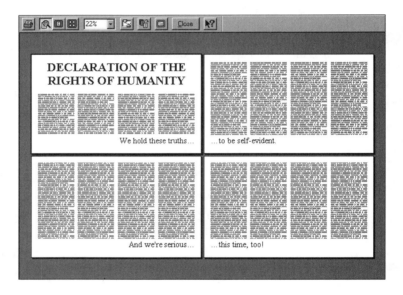

3. Use the buttons on the Preview screen to get a better look at your document.

- Click the Zoom Control menu and enter or choose a different percentage setting to see more of a page. You can also click the Page Width setting to make the page wider on the Preview screen.

- Click the Shrink to Fit button, and Word 95 shrinks your document a bit. Choose this option if the last page has only a few lines of text and you want to save a piece of paper.

- The Full Screen button removes the menu bars and ruler so that you can really get the "big picture" of a page.

- Click the Magnifier button to zoom in on a part of a page. When you click this button, a magnifying glass cursor appears. Click the part of the document you want to examine. When you're done, click again to get back to the Preview screen.

Shrinks document

Shows one page   Closes Preview screen

Prints the document   Shrinks pages

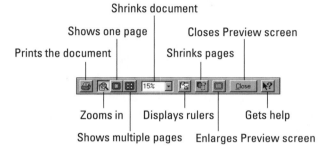

Zooms in   Displays rulers   Gets help

Shows multiple pages   Enlarges Preview screen

4. Click <u>C</u>lose if you need to go back to the document and make changes; otherwise, click the Print button.

Printing Addresses on Envelopes

You don't have to address envelopes by hand, although it's often easier to do it that way. Here's how to print delivery addresses and return addresses on envelopes:

1. Open the document that holds the letter you want to send. The name and address of the person you're sending the letter to should be at the top of the document. If it isn't, enter it.

2. Select the name and address of the person you want to send the letter to.

3. Choose <u>T</u>ools⇨<u>E</u>nvelopes and Labels. The Envelopes and Labels dialog box appears with the address you selected in the <u>D</u>elivery Address box. Your address should appear in the <u>R</u>eturn Address box (if it isn't there, see the Tip at the end of this entry to find out how to put it there).

4. Change the <u>D</u>elivery Address or <u>R</u>eturn Address if necessary.

5. Click the O<u>m</u>it button if you don't want your return address to appear on the envelope.

6. Click the <u>P</u>rint button.

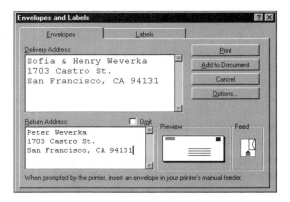

Two commands on the Envelopes and Labels dialog box tell Word 95 how your printer handles envelopes and what size your envelopes are.

Click the envelope in the Feed area to choose the right technique for feeding envelopes to your printer. Click one of the Feed Method boxes, click the Face Up or Face Down option button, and pull down the Feed From menu to tell Word 95 which printer tray the envelope is in or how you intend to stick the envelope in your printer.

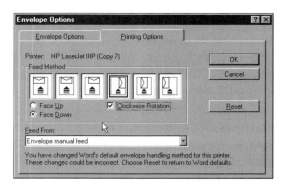

After you feed the envelope to your printer, click either the Options button or the Preview box on the Envelopes and Labels dialog box to tell Word 95 what size your envelopes are. Choose other settings, too:

✦ **Envelope Size:** Pull down the menu and select the right size.

✦ **Delivery Point Bar Code:** Click here to put bar codes on the envelope and help the post office deliver the letter faster.

✦ **FIM-A Courtesy Reply Mail:** Click here to put Facing Identification Marks on the envelope. These marks, which tell letter processing machines at the post office whether the envelope is face up, also help with the speedy delivery of mail.

✦ **Delivery Address Font:** Change the font of the delivery address.

✦ **Return Address Font:** Ditto for the return address.

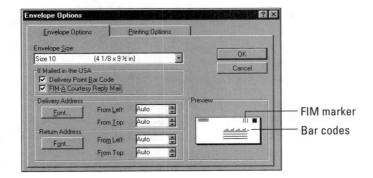

FIM marker

Bar codes

That Add to Document button on the Envelopes and Labels dialog box creates a new section at the top of the document with the return and delivery address in it. In the new section, both addresses are formatted and made ready to go straight to the printer. Not everyone can take advantage of this feature. Click the Add to Document button only if you have a printer that can accept envelopes as easily as it can accept sheets of paper (I want one for my birthday).

To make your return address appear automatically in the Return Address box, choose Tools⊏⊃Options, click the User Info tab, and enter your name and address in the Mailing Address box.

Printing on Different-Sized Paper

You don't have to print exclusively on standard 8.5 x 11 paper; you can print on legal-size paper and other sizes of paper as well.

To change the size of the paper on which you intend to print a document:

1. Choose File⊏⊃Page Setup.

2. Click the Paper Size tab.

3. Choose a setting from the Paper Size drop-down list. If none of the settings suits you, enter your own settings in the Width and Height text boxes.

4. Choose an Apply To option:

• **Whole Document** for the entire document

- **This Section** if your document has more than one section

- **This Point Forward** to create a new section and change the paper size for the rest of the document

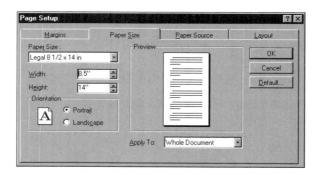

5. Click OK.

If you keep legal-size paper in one tray of your printer and standard-size paper in another, for example, click the Paper Source tab in the Page Setup dialog box and change settings there.

 Click the Default button in the Page Setup dialog box if you want your choice of paper size to be the default — the choice that is made whenever you open a new document.

Printing a Document

 The fastest way to print a document is to click the Print button on the toolbar (shown at left). Go this route if you want to print the entire thing from start to finish. (Before you print a document, however, you ought to "preview" it by pressing the Print Preview button or choosing File⇨Print Preview.)

To print part of a document, selected text in a document, the entire thing, or even unusual things like annotations and summary text:

1. Choose File⇨Print (or press Ctrl+P).

2. Choose a Print Range option to tell Word 95 how much of the document to print:

- **All:** Prints the whole thing.

- **Current page:** Prints only the page where the cursor is.

- **Selection:** Prints the text that is highlighted.

- **Pages:** Prints certain pages only. Enter hyphens to designate

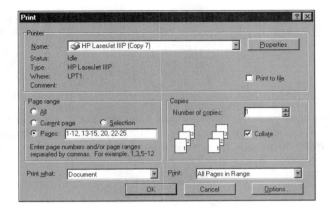

the page range and commas too if you want to print more than one page range. For example, entering **1–4** prints pages 1 through 4, but entering **1,4** prints only those pages.

3. Choose Print to file to copy the document to a print file. You might do this in order to take your document to a print shop and have it printed there. If you choose this option and click OK, the Print to File dialog box appears. Choose a name for the print file and click OK.

4. Enter the number of copies you want in the Number of copies box.

5. Click OK.

The Print dialog box also offers these options:

✦ **Collate:** If you're printing more than one copy of a document with many pages and don't want the copies to be collated, click the Collate box to remove the check mark. If you were printing three three-page documents, for example, the pages would come out of the printer 111, 222, 333, instead of 123, 123, 123.

✦ **Print what:** Choose one of the admittedly strange options on the Print what drop-down menu to print the annotations in your document, AutoText entries, examples of the styles you've used, key assignments you've used, or file summary information.

✦ **Print:** Choose Odd Pages or Even Pages from the Print menu to print those pages only.

Printing Labels

You can print pages of labels in Word 95, and single labels, too.

Needless to say, printing labels makes mass mailing and bulk mailing much easier. If you have Avery brand labels, you've got it made, because Word 95 is all set up to work with Avery labels.

As much as it pains me to write this, you should probably get a box of Avery labels if you want to print labels with Word 95 (although the program does offer some precustomized settings for use with European paper-size standards). You can tell Word 95 what your labels look like by fiddling with the settings, but one peek at the Preview box that you use to do so will probably discourage you from even thinking about it:

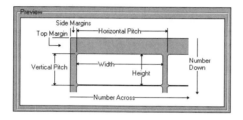

Printing labels one at a time

To print mailing labels:

1. Open the document that contains the address that you want to print on the label and select the address.

2. Choose Tools⇨Envelopes and Labels.

3. Click the Labels tab. The address appears in the Address box. If the name or address is wrong, now's the time to fix it. If you're printing labels with your return address on them, click the Use Return Address box or enter your return address.

4. Either choose Options or click the sample label in the Label box. The Label Options dialog box appears.

5. In the Printer Information area, click either Dot Matrix or Laser to tell Word which kind of printer you have. Then pull down the Tray menu and click the option that describes how you will feed the label to your printer.

6. Click the Label Products drop-down list and choose the brand of labels you have — Avery Standard, Avery A4 Sizes, or Other.

You may not have to choose Other if you don't have Avery labels. You might be able to choose an Avery line similar to the labels you have (see step 7). If you do choose Other, click the Details button and use the Custom Information dialog box to explain, in 4,000 words or less, how your labels are laid out on the page.

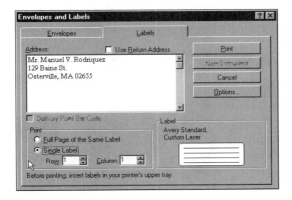

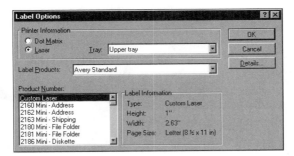

7. In the Product Number box, click the Avery product you have. If you don't have Avery labels, click the various kinds of Avery labels and look in the Label Information box on the right to see if the Height, Width, and Page Size match those of the labels you have. If they do, you can choose an Avery label.

8. Click OK to go back to the Envelopes and Labels dialog box.

9. Choose a Print option:

- **Full Page of the Same Label:** Click this box if you want to print a pageful of the same label. Likely, you'd choose this option to print a pageful of your own return addresses. Click the New Document button after you make this choice, and then save and print this document.

- **Single Label:** Click this box to print one label. Then enter the row and column where the label is and click the Print button.

Printing labels for mass mailings

If you want to print a mess of labels for mass or bulk mailings, use the Mail Merge Helper. Before you do that, however, you have to get your mailing list into some kind of shape that Word 95 can recognize. If you don't have a mailing list, Word 95 gives you an opportunity to make one as part of the mail merge.

If you already have a mailing list on disk, you can open it and use it to print labels. You have to do some fiddling around, however. First, put the same number of rows in each address. In other words, if some of your addresses have four lines and others have three, add a fourth, blank line to the addresses with only three lines. Then take the paragraph symbols (the ¶ symbols in your list that appear when you press Enter) out of your list and replace them with tabs, all except after the last line of addresses. To see paragraph symbols, click the Show/Hide ¶ button on the toolbar.

```
Mr.·Manuel·V.·Rodriquez → 129·Bains·St. → Osterville,·MA·02655¶
Ms.·Gladys·Yee→1289·Durham·Lane → Osterville,·MA→02655¶
Mr.·Clyde·T.·Haines→1293·Durham·Lane → Osterville,·MA·02655¶
Ms.·Esther·Harmony→2601·Estner·Rd. → Osterville,·MA·02655¶
Ms.·Melinda·Sings → 2789·Estner·Rd. → Osterville,·MA→02655¶
```

Note: If you haven't typed names for the labels yet, *see* "Form(ing) Letters" in Part V. It explains how to enter your own names and addresses so that Word can use them for mailing lists and form letters.

It's impossible to create completely clean labels from a list, but it helps to use tabs. Save and close your address list, and don't forget its name.

Now you're ready to use the Mail Merge Helper to create a file of address labels:

1. Open a new document and choose Tools⇨Mail Merge. The Mail Merge Helper opens.

2. Click the Create button and then click Mailing Labels in the drop-down list.

3. In the message box, click Active window to add the labels to the new document you just opened.

4. Under step 2 in the Mail Merge Helper, click Get Data and choose Open Data Source from the drop-down list. You can also get labels from your personal address book or the Microsoft Scheduler+ application by choosing those options. (If you were creating the labels from scratch, you would choose Get Data from the drop-down list in this step.)

5. In the Open Data Source dialog box, find the document that contains your addresses, click it, and click the Open button.

6. Click Merge under Step 3 of the Mail Merge Helper.

7. In the Header Record Delimiters dialog box, Tab should already be the choice in the Field Delimiter box. In the Record Delimiter box, ¶ (enter) should be the choice. If either is not already the choice in these boxes, put it there and click OK.

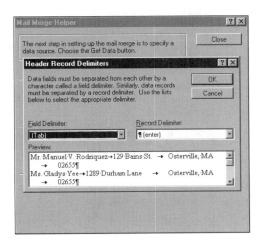

8. In the message box that appears, click the Set Up Main Document button.

9. Choose options in the Label Options dialog box. If these options are new to you, consult steps 5 through 7 in the preceding section of this part. Click OK when you're done. The Create Labels dialog box appears.

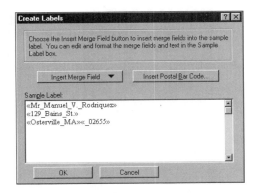

10. This dialog box is where you create the sample label that Word 95 uses as model for all the labels on the list. Place the cursor in the Sample Label box where you want the addressee's name to go, click Insert Merge Field, and choose the name from the drop-down list. It appears in the Sample Label box.

11. Press Enter to go to the next line, click Insert Merge Field again, and enter the next line in the address, probably the street number and name. Press Enter again. Keep doing this until you enter the entire address.

12. Fix all punctuation, remove empty spaces and enter blank ones where necessary, put a blank space before the ZIP code (to separate it from the two-letter state abbreviation), and do whatever else is necessary to clean up the address. Microsoft Weird 95 stripped out all my punctuation (commas and periods), and I had to re-enter it. It also put mysterious *M*s in the list.

Whatever you do, don't erase the angle brackets (<<>>) or press Enter inside them. They mark off the parts of the address.

13. Click OK. The Merge dialog box appears.

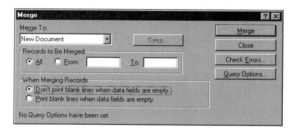

Make sure that the Don't print blank lines when data fields are empty box is checked. This prevents blank lines from appearing in your labels.

14. Click OK. Word 95 generates the mailing labels in a file called Labels1 and you get something like this:

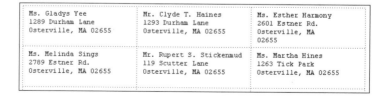

15. Go into the list and clean it up.

16. Choose File⇨Save, press Ctrl+S, or click the Save button and save your label file under a new name in the Save As dialog box.

17. Now that your labels are on disk, put a blank sheet of labels in the printer and print your new labels.

See also "Form(ing) Letters" in Part V.

Solving Problems with the Printer

Occasionally, you try to print a document and get this disconcerting message or one like it:

In David Letterman fashion, here is a top-ten list of things to do when you can't print a document or a document doesn't print correctly:

10. Is text running off the page? You may have attempted to print on paper that is the wrong size. Choose File⇨Printer Setup, click the Paper Size tab, and change the Paper Size options.

9. Are your graphics not printing? Choose Tools⇨Options, click the Print tab, and deselect the Draft Output check box.

8. You can't choose the Print command on the File menu because it's dimmed? You may have selected the wrong printer. Choose File⇨Print and choose another printer from the Name drop-down list. If that doesn't work, try reinstalling your printer with the Add New Hardware application in the Windows 95 Control Panel.

7. The gridlines don't appear in tables? That's because you haven't put borders on your table or you're printing on a dot-matrix printer, which doesn't print table lines very well.

6. You've loaded envelopes in the printer but Word 95 still doesn't budge? You probably put the envelopes in the wrong tray. Choose Tools⇨Envelopes and Labels, click the Envelopes tab, click the Options button, and choose the correct method of loading envelopes in your printer.

5. Do fonts look different on-screen than they do on paper? Your printer might not be able to handle certain fonts, in which case you have to find substitutes among the TrueType fonts you have (they have TT next to their names).

4. Are lines breaking in strange places? Your margins may be too wide. Change the margin settings.

3. You keep seeing the `There is an error writing to your printer` message? You may have sent too many print jobs to the printer. Wait for your printer to digest what you've already sent it and try again.

2. Does Word 95 tell you `There was an error writing to blah blah blah`? You may be out of paper.

1. Are you getting nothing but error messages? See if the printer is turned on. If it's not on, you can't print.

Telling Word 95 How to Print Documents

To print a document, Word 95 has to know where the paper is and what kind of printer you're using. And if you keep different paper in different trays, you need to tell Word 95 where the right size paper is.

1. Choose File⇨Print or press Ctrl+P.

2. In the Print dialog box, click the down arrow on the Name drop-down menu and choose a printer, if necessary.

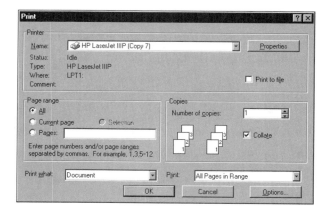

3. Click the Properties button.

4. On the Paper tab, choose which size paper you're using or which size envelope you intend to print on.

5. From the paper Source drop-down list, choose the right tray, or choose a method of feeding envelopes to your printer if you're printing an envelope.

6. Click OK to get back to the Print dialog box and click OK again.

Making Your Work Go Faster

Computers are supposed to make your work easier and faster. And if you can cut through all the jargon and technobabble, they can really do that.

Part V explains shortcuts and commands that will help you become a speedy user of Word 95. Everything in this part of the book was put here so that you can get off work an hour earlier and take the slow, scenic route home.

In this part...

- ✓ **Moving around quickly in long documents**
- ✓ **Creating form letters by merging letters with names and addresses in a database**
- ✓ **Linking files**
- ✓ **Entering data quickly with forms**
- ✓ **Using master documents and outlines to organize your work**
- ✓ **Customizing Word 95 so that it works for you**

Bookmarks for Hopping Around

Instead of pressing PgUp or PgDn or using the scrollbars to thrash around in a long document, you can use bookmarks. All you do is put a bookmark in an important spot in your document that you'll return to many times. When you want to return to that spot, choose Edit⇔Bookmark and double-click the bookmark in the Bookmark dialog box.

This mystery writer, true to the craft, wrote the end of the story first and used bookmarks to jump back and forth between the beginning and end to make all the clues fit together:

To place a bookmark in a document:

1. Click where you want the bookmark to go.

2. Choose Edit⇔Bookmark (or press Ctrl+Shift+F5).

3. Type a descriptive name in the text box. You cannot include spaces in bookmark names.

4. Click the Add button.

To go to a bookmark:

1. Choose Edit⇔Bookmark.

2. Double-click the bookmark, or select it and click the Go To button.

You can arrange bookmarks in the list in alphabetical order or by location in the document by choosing an option button at the bottom of the Bookmark dialog box.

To delete a bookmark, select it in the Bookmark dialog box and click the Delete button.

TIP

You can see where bookmarks are in your document. Choose
Tools⇔Options, click the View tab, and click the Bookmarks check
box. Then click the Show/Hide ¶ button. A boldface symbol that looks
like a capital *I* appears where bookmarks are.

Correcting Typos on the Fly

COOL STUFF

Unless you or someone else has messed with Word 95's AutoCorrect
settings, the invisible hand of Word 95 corrects certain typos as you
enter them. Try misspelling *weird* by typing *wierd* to see what I mean.
Try entering two hyphens (- -) and you get an em dash (—). You can
have Word 95 correct the typos you make often, and with a little
cunning you can even use the AutoCorrect feature to enter long
company names and hard-to-spell names on the fly.

To change the settings and make AutoCorrect work for you, choose
Tools⇔AutoCorrect. The AutoCorrect dialog box appears.

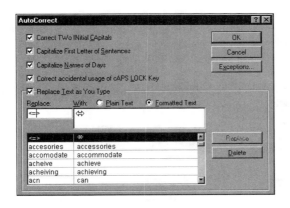

+ Remove the check marks from the AutoCorrect features you
  don't want. For example, if you enter a lot of computer code in
  your manuscripts, you don't necessarily want the first letter of
  sentences to be capitalized automatically, so you should click the
  Capitalize First Letter of Sentences check box to deselect it.

+ If you want, remove the check mark from the Replace Text As
  You Type box to keep Word's invisible hand from correcting
  capitalization idiosyncrasies as you enter them.

+ Scroll through the list and take a look at the words that are
  "autocorrected." If you don't want a word on the list to be
  corrected, select it and click Delete.

+ If a word that you misspell often isn't on the list, you can add it
  to the list and have Word 95 correct it automatically. Enter the

misspelling in the Replace box, enter the right spelling in the With box, and click the Add button.

✦ If you don't like one of Word 95's replacement words, select the word on the list, enter a new replacement word in the With box, and click the Replace button.

Click OK when you're done.

The Spelling dialog box has an AutoCorrect button. Click it when you're spell-checking a document to add the word you're correcting to the list of words that are "autocorrected."

If AutoCorrect frustrates you, you don't have to ditch it altogether. You can have Word make exceptions for the words, proper names, and abbreviations you use. For example, if you work for QUestdata Corp., you can make Word allow that name to stand but still correct other instances where you type two capital letters in a row. If you use a certain abbreviation often, you can add it to the list of abbreviations that Word 95 lets stand without starting the next word with a capital letter. Here's how:

1. Choose Tools➪AutoCorrect.

2. Click the Exceptions button.

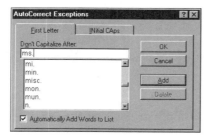

3. On the First Letter tab, enter abbreviations that you intend to use but that aren't on the list. Word capitalizes the first letter after a period, except in the cases of the abbreviations listed here.

4. On the INitial CAps tab, enter words or names with two capitals in a row that you want Word to let stand.

5. Click OK twice to get back to your document.

With a little cunning, you can use AutoCorrect to enter long words, long e-mail addresses, and the like. Suppose you are writing the definitive work on Gaetano Donizetti, the Italian opera composer. To keep from having to type his long name over and over, choose

Tools⇨AutoCorrect, enter **/gd** (or something similar) in the Replace box, enter the full name in the With box, and click OK. Now all you have to do is type **/gd** and a blank space, and AutoCorrect does the rest. The catch is that you have to enter letters in the Replace box that you won't ever, ever, ever need to really use.

Customizing Word 95

You can make Word 95 work your way by fiddling with the commands in the Options dialog box. You can even put menu commands in different places and invent your own keyboard shortcuts for executing commands. *See* "Rearranging the Toolbars," also in this part, to see how to make toolbars with your favorite command buttons on them.

One glance at the 12 tabs in the Options dialog box tells you that there is a lot to fiddle with. You can see this dialog box by choosing Tools⇨Options. If you decide to play around with these options, do so carefully because you might change a setting, forget where you changed it, and not be able to change it back again.

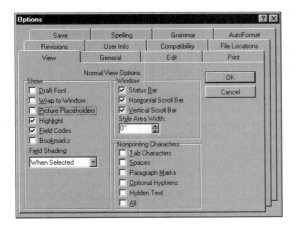

Changing the menu commands

You can decide for yourself which menu commands appear on which menus. You can also add macros, fonts, AutoText entries, and styles to menus. Doing so is easy, and if you make a mistake and want to go back to the original menus, that is easy, too.

The quickest way to remove a command from a menu is to press Ctrl+Alt+hyphen. When the cursor changes into an ominous black bar, simply select the menu command you want to remove and Bob's your uncle.

To remove menu commands or alter the menus, use the Menus tab of the Customize dialog box:

1. Choose Tools⇨Customize.

2. Click the Menus tab.

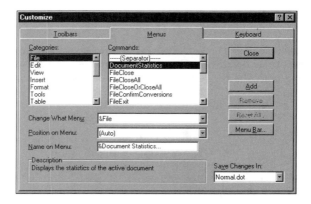

3. If you want to make the menu changes to a template other than the one in the Save Changes In drop-down list, choose it.

4. In the Categories list, select the menu you want to change. If you're adding a macro, font, AutoText entry, or style to a menu, scroll to the bottom of the Categories list and select it.

5. Choose the command you're changing in the Commands list.

6. Choose the menu you want to move the command to in the Change What Menu drop-down list.

7. In the Position on Menu drop-down list, say where the menu command should go:

- **Auto:** With similar commands on the menu

- **At Top:** At the beginning

- **At bottom:** At the end

- **Other Commands:** Directly below a menu command that you select

8. If you want, enter a new name for the command in the Name on Menu box. To create a hot key for the command, enter **&** before the hot key character.

9. Click Add.

10. Click Close.

If you wish that you hadn't messed with the menus and want to repent, go back to the Menus tab of the Customize dialog box and click Reset All. Answer Yes when Word 95 asks whether you want to get the old menus back.

Changing the keyboard shortcuts

If you don't like Word 95's keyboard shortcuts, you can change them and invent keyboard shortcuts of your own. You can also assign keyboard shortcuts to symbols, macros, fonts, AutoText entries, and styles.

1. Choose Tools⊅Customize.

2. Click the Keyboard tab.

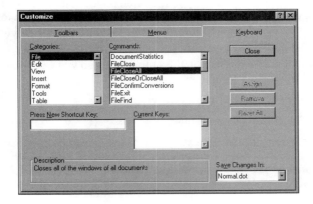

3. If necessary, choose a template in the Save Changes In drop-down list.

4. In the Categories list, choose the menu in which you want to assign the keyboard shortcut. At the bottom of the list are the Macro, Font, AutoText, Style, and Symbols categories.

5. Choose the command name, macro, font, AutoText entry, style, or symbol name in the Commands list.

6. Click in the Press New Shortcut Key box and type the keyboard shortcut. Press the actual keys. For example, if the shortcut is Ctrl+Z, press the Ctrl key and the Z key — don't type out **C-t-r-l-+-Z**.

If you try to assign a shortcut that is already assigned, the words Currently Assigned To and a command name appear below the Press New Shortcut Key box. You can override the preassigned keyboard assignment by entering a keyboard assignment of your own.

7. Click the Assign button.

8. When you're done, click the Close button.

To delete a keyboard shortcut, display it in the Current Keys box, click it to select it, and click the Remove button.

 You can always get the old keyboard shortcuts back by choosing the Reset All button on the Keyboard tab of the Customize dialog box. Click Yes when Word 95 asks whether you really want the old keyboard shortcuts back.

Entering Graphics and Text Quickly

 Put the text and graphics you use often on the AutoText list. That way, you can enter the text or graphics simply by clicking a few menu commands. Addresses and company logos are ideal candidates for the AutoText list.

To put text or a graphic on the AutoText list so you can enter it quickly:

1. Type the text or import the graphic.

2. Select the text or graphic.

3. Choose Edit⇨AutoText. The AutoText dialog box appears:

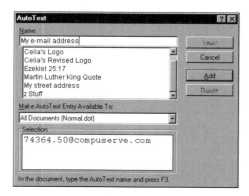

4. Type a name for the text or graphic in the Name box.

5. If you want your new AutoText entry to be available only when you're working in certain templates, drop down the Make AutoText Entry Available To menu and choose a template.

6. Glance in the Selection box to make sure that you're adding the right text or graphic to the list and click the Add button.

The fastest way to enter an AutoText entry is to place the cursor where you want it to go, type the entry's name, and press F3.

You can also enter text or a graphic from the AutoText name list:

1. Place the cursor where you want the text or graphic to appear.

2. Choose Edit⇨AutoText.

3. Click a name on the Name list. You may have to scroll down the list to get to the name you want.

4. Click the Insert button.

To delete an AutoText entry from the list, select it and click the Delete button.

Entering Information Quickly with Forms

A *form* is simply a means of soliciting and recording information. Using Word 95, you can create computerized forms that make entering data easy. Designing forms is a tricky business and is too complicated for this little book, but this entry will get you started.

To see how forms work, suppose you are the president of a PTA. You would like to get information from other PTA members, so you create paper forms for members to fill out at the first meeting. Once the information is in hand, you can enter it cleanly and quickly in Word 95 on a computerized form.

First, create the paper form you'll hand out at the PTA meeting. It might look like this:

Oklahoma City Arts High School

Welcome to our first PTA meeting. To help with the volunteer effort, please fill out the form below and leave it at the door on the way out.

Student's Name	First:	Last:	
Parents' Names	First:	Last:	
Phone Number	Home:	Work:	
Address	Street:	City:	Zip:

Volunteer hours per week (circle one): 1   3   6   8

I can volunteer in these areas:

When the meeting is over and you have the information in hand, you have to turn your paper form into a computerized one. The first step is to turn the form into a template:

1. Open the document with the form on it. You might enter some sample data to see how lines break when you enter data on the form. Format the text to make it easy for the data-entry person to enter the data. You can also delete text that isn't necessary. For example, in the sample document shown here, you would delete "Oklahoma City Arts High School."

2. Choose File⇨Save As.

3. Type a name for the template in the File name box.

4. Click the Up One Level button until you get to the Templates folder.

5. Choose Document Template in the Save as type drop-down list. The name of your template should have a *.dot* ending.

6. Click Save.

Now that the form is a template, you have to put input fields in it so that you or another volunteer can enter data from the forms you've collected. A *field* is simply a piece of information. In the volunteer form example, there are 11 input fields. Input fields fall into three categories:

✦ **Text:** A text entry, such as a name, address, or telephone number. Ten fields in the sample template are text fields.

✦ **Check Box:** A "multiple choice," such as the question that asks about the number of volunteer hours in the sample template.

✦ **Drop Down:** A drop-down menu of choices.

To enter input field types, you can use either the Insert⇨Form Field command or the Forms toolbar. To use the Forms toolbar, choose View⇨Toolbars and click the Forms check box to display the toolbar on-screen. To enter the input fields:

1. Go to the first place in the template where data is to be entered.

2. Choose Insert⇨Form Field and click one of the Type option buttons in the Form Field dialog box. Or else click the Text Form Field, Check Box Form Field, or Drop-Down Form Field button on the Forms toolbar.

3. Keep going down the template and entering form fields.

4. Click the Form Field Shading button on the Forms toolbar to get a better idea of where the fields are. Don't worry about their length. Unless you click the Options button on the Form Field dialog box or the Form Field Options button on the toolbar and change the settings, you can enter text of any length in input fields. You might change the length setting in a zip code field to keep anyone from inputting more than nine numbers, for example.

 5. When you're done entering the input fields, click the Protect from button. Now whoever enters the data on the form cannot disturb the field names. He or she can only type in the input fields. Your template looks something like this:

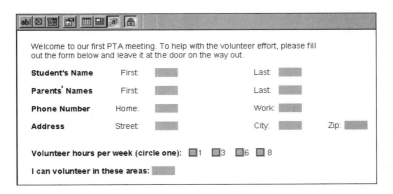

6. Save the template and close it.

Now that you have the template, you can enter data cleanly in easy-to-read forms:

1. Choose File⇨New to open a new document to enter the data in.

2. Double-click the template you created.

3. Enter information in the input fields. Press the up or down arrow or press Tab and Shift+Tab to move from field to field. You can also click input fields to move the cursor there.

4. When you're done, either print the document or save it.

Form (ing) Letters

Thanks to the miracle of computing, you can churn out form letters in the privacy of your home or office, just like the big companies do. To create form letters, you complete three steps:

1. Create the *main document,* the document with the actual text of the letter.

2. Create the *source document,* the document with the names, addresses, and any other text that differs from letter to letter.

3. Merge the two documents to generate the form letters.

To generate form letters:

1. Open a new document by clicking the New button, pressing Ctrl+N, or choosing File⇨New. With the File⇨New command, you can choose one of Word 95's letter templates for your form letter.

2. Choose Tools⇨Mail Merge. The Mail Merge Helper dialog box appears.

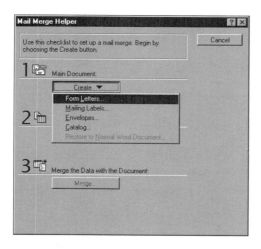

3. Click the Create button and choose Form Letters from the drop-down list.

4. Choose Active Document window when Word asks you which window you want to use to create the form letters. The active document window becomes the *source document.*

5. Back at the Mail Merge Helper, click the Get Data button and choose Create Data Source.

If you want to use names and addresses from the Address Book for the form letters, click Use Address Book. You can also use a data source of your own if you already have a name and address database. *See* "Printing labels for mass mailings" in Part IV to find out how to do this.

The Create Data Source dialog box appears. This is where you tell Word 95 which fields to include in the form letter. In computerese, a *field* is simply one piece of information. For example, your name and address include at least six fields: first name, last name, street number and name, city, state, and postal code.

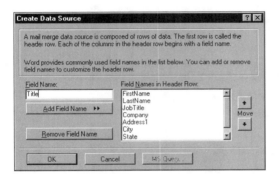

6. In the Field Names in Header Row box, click each field you *don't* need and then click the Remove Field Name button.

Carefully consider which fields your form letter requires and look in the Field Names in Header Row box to see which fields you need. Likely, your form letter needs the FirstName, LastName, Address1, City, State, and PostalCode fields. You can include others if you want to.

7. To add a field of your own, type its name in the Field Name text box and click the Add Field Name button.

8. Arrange the field names in the Field Names in Header Row box in the order in which they'll appear in your form letter. To do so, highlight a field and press one of the Move buttons to move the field to the right place.

9. Click OK to close the Create Data Source dialog box.

10. In the Save As dialog box, enter a name for your *data source* document in the File name text box. This is the document where you store all the information that changes from form letter to form letter. Then click Save.

11. Word tells you that you need to add records to the data source document you just named. Click the Edit Data Source button. The

Data Form dialog box appears with the names of the fields you created in the Create Data Source dialog box.

12. Enter data in each field. If you need to leave a field blank, leave it blank — don't put any blank spaces in it.

13. Click the Add New button to enter the next name and address. When you're done entering all of them, click OK.

Now you see the *main document* again. This is where you type the text of the form letter.

14. Start typing the letter. When you come to a place where you want to insert a field, click the Insert Merge Field button and choose the field from the list.

15. Keep typing and making field selections with the Insert Field Merge button. You can format the letter any way you wish. It will look something like the following figure when you're done.

16. When you're done, click the Mail Merge Helper button.

17. In the now-familiar Mail Merge Helper dialog box, click the Merge button. The Merge dialog box appears as shown in the second figure on the next page.

Click here when you're done

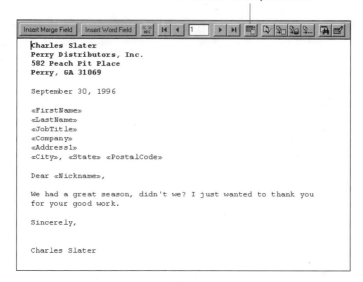

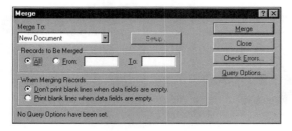

18. In the Merge dialog box, tell Word 95 how to merge the *data source* with the *main document:*

- **Merge To:** Choose New Document to create a new file with all the form letters in it. If you're generating a lot of form letters, this file can get very large. Choose Print to merge the names and addresses with the form letter as the form letters are printed. This choice requires less disk space.

- **Records to Be Merged:** Click All or else enter a record number in the From and To boxes.

- **When Merging Records:** This option pertains to merging addresses on labels, not to form letters, so you can ignore it.

- **Check Errors:** Click this button, and Word 95 reports errors as the files are merged. For example, it tells you when it can't find

a match between the data source and a field in your form
letter.

- **Query Options:** Opens a dialog box so you can sort
  (rearrange) or filter (weed out) records. Click this option, for
  example, to merge the letters in a different order (perhaps in
  zip code order) or merge only addresses in a certain state or
  zip code.

19. Click OK in the Merge dialog box.

20. If you choose to merge to the printer in step 18, the Print dialog
box appears so that you can choose settings and print away. If
you choose New Document, Word 95 creates a new document
with the name Form Letters1. Look over the form letters for
mistakes and perhaps enter a few chummy, personal comments
before you print the document.

21. Sign and mail the form letters. Use Elvis stamps if you can
find them.

Going Here, Going There in Documents

One fast way to go from place to place in a document is to use the
Edit⇨Go To command. Choose this command or press Ctrl+G to see
the Go To dialog box:

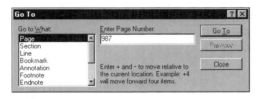

The Go to What menu in this dialog box lists everything that can
conceivably be numbered in a Word 95 document, plus bookmarks.
Click a menu item and enter a number to go elsewhere. In the case
of bookmarks, choose Bookmarks and select a bookmark from the
drop-down list on the right side of the dialog box.

Click the Previous button to go back to the footnote, endnote,
annotation, line, or whatever you just came from. You can press + or –
and enter numbers to go backward or forward by one or several
numbered items at once.

Here's another quick way to jump around in documents:

1. Switch to Outline view.

2. Click in the heading you want to go.

3. Switch back to Normal or Page Layout view and press the up-arrow or down-arrow key.

Inserting Automatic Information in Documents

A *field* represents information that varies. The best way to see what fields do is to choose Insert⇨Field and examine the many different fields in the Field dialog box. In the Categories list, click a field that piques your interest, click a name in the Field Names list, and read the description at the bottom of the dialog box. You can also click the ? button in the dialog box and click in the Field Codes box to find out more about a field you've selected.

Here are the Date and Time fields:

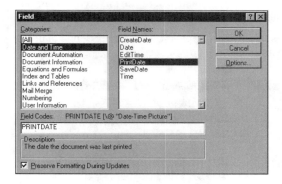

To insert a field:

1. Place the cursor where you want the field to go.

2. Choose Insert⇨Field.

3. Select a field by choosing a category and name.

4. Click the Options button and choose how you want to present the field. Which options you see depends on the field you choose in step 3. If you choose Date, for example, you see different formats for presenting the date: *M/d/yy* gets you 9/17/96, for example; *dddd, mmmm dd, yyyy* gets you Monday, September 17, 1996. Choose the format you want in the Field Options dialog box, click Add to Field, and click OK.

5. Click OK.

Linking Documents to Save on Work

You can save a lot of time and effort by connecting two documents so that changes made to the first are made automatically to the second. This process is called *linking*. If a table in a memo you're working on happens to be useful in an annual report as well, you can link the documents, and updates to the table in the memo will show up in the annual report whenever you save the memo.

Creating a link

To link documents this way:

1. Open the document with the text you want to link.

 2. Select the text and copy it to the Clipboard by clicking the Copy button, pressing Ctrl+C, or choosing Edit⇨Copy.

3. Switch to the document where the linked text is to be pasted and put the cursor where you want the text to go.

4. Choose Edit⇨Paste Special. The Paste Special dialog box appears.

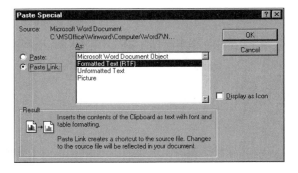

5. Click the Paste Link option button.

6. If the thing being linked is not text, choose Microsoft Word Document Object, Unformatted Text, or Picture in the As box.

7. Click Display as Icon if you'd like the text to appear as an icon in the document. If you make this choice, you create a *manual link.* Manual links are updated only when you tell Word 95 to update them. *Automatic links,* on the other hand, are updated whenever you make changes to the original text. If you choose Display as Icon to create a manual link, a Change Icon button appears so that you can choose the icon that is used in the text to show where the manual link has been made.

8. Click OK.

This figure shows two links in a document: a manual link and an automatic link. The manual link is represented by an icon. When I clicked the automatic link, the text changed to gray to show that it was put here with the Edit⇨Paste Special command.

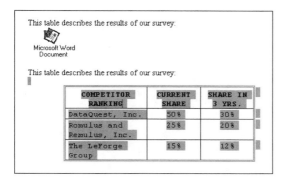

TIP

To convert a Microsoft Word Document icon into the original text that it represents, select the icon, choose Edit⇨Linked Document Object⇨Convert, click the Display as Icon box, and click OK. Do the same to change text into an icon but remove the check mark from the Display as Icon box.

Updating, breaking, and changing links

As I mentioned, changes made with automatic links are made to the linked document whenever a change is made to the original text. With manual links, however, you have to tell Word 95 to update the link.

FAST TRACK

The fast way to do that is to right-click the linked text and choose Update Link from the shortcut menu:

You can also update a link — and do other things besides — from the Links dialog box:

1. Choose Edit➪Links.

2. In the Links dialog box, select the link you want to update. Be sure to look at the Source File listing at the bottom of the dialog box to make sure that you're updating the right link.

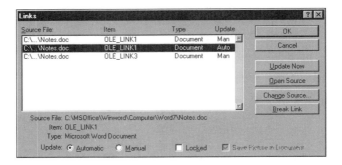

3. Click the Update Now button.

4. Click OK.

You can update several links at once by Ctrl+clicking the links before you click the Update Now button.

The Links dialog box offers several more buttons and check boxes for handling links:

✦ **Open Source:** Opens the original document so that you can make changes to text.

✦ **Change Source:** If you move the original document to another folder, Word 95 doesn't know where to look for the document that contains the original text. Click this button to open the Change Source dialog box. Then find the original document and click Open. The link is re-established.

✦ **Break Link:** Severs the tie between the original document and the document with the link in it. Once you click this button, the link is broken, and you can't get it back.

✦ **Automatic:** Changes the link to an automatic link.

✦ **Manual:** Changes the link to a manual link.

✦ **Locked:** Makes it so updates to the original document do not affect the linked document. Choose this option instead of Break Link if you want to break the link but still be able to go to the original document if you have to.

✦ **Save Picture in Document:** Saves the link in your document as a "picture." This option is for use with graphics and is designed to save disk space. Instead of saving the computer code used to create the graphic, Word 95 saves a picture of the graphic.

Suppose you're in the linked document and you realize that you need to change the original text. If the link is a manual one, all you have to do is double-click the Microsoft Word Document icon to get to the original text. With an automatic link, choose Edit➪Linked Document Object➪Open, or right-click and choose Open Document Link from the shortcut menu.

To make sure that all links are updated before you print documents, choose Tools➪Options, click the Print tab, and click the Update Links box.

If you delete the original file, that's the end of your link. You can't get it back. So long, Charlie.

Macros

A *macro* is a set of instructions that you can give with a single command. Macros help automate difficult and long-winded tasks. After you create a macro, you can put it on a menu, put it on a toolbar, or assign it a keyboard shortcut to make it easy to execute.

Macros can get very complex, and changing a macro after you record it is difficult indeed. This book isn't long enough to explore the whole world of macros. I'll just show you how to record and run a macro.

Recording a macro

To record a macro:

1. Double-click the REC button on the status bar or choose Tools➪Macro and click the Record button. The Record Macro dialog box appears.

2. Type a name for the macro in the Record Macro Name box. You can't include spaces between the letters in the name.

3. Enter a description in the Description box.

4. If you want your macro to be available only in certain templates, choose one or more templates from the Make Macro Available To drop-down list.

5. If you want to be able to run your macro with a keyboard shortcut or from a toolbar or menu, choose Toolbars, Menus, or Keyboard. The Customize dialog box opens so that you can add

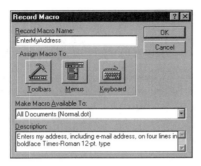

the macro name to a toolbar or menu or designate a keyboard shortcut for activating the macro. (*See* "Rearranging the Toolbars" and "Customizing Word 95," also in this part, if you need help completing this step.)

6. Click OK in the Record Macro dialog box. Word 95 sends you back to your document, where the cursor has changed into a cassette tape and the Macro Record toolbar has arrived on the scene.

Click to stop recording

Click to pause

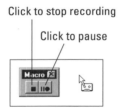

7. Very carefully enter the commands and type the text for your macro. You can choose commands with the mouse, but you can't select text, copy text, or drag and drop text with the mouse. Click the Pause button if you need to stop recording for a moment to give commands or take a coffee break. Click it again when you're ready to resume.

8. After you're done recording the macro, click the Stop button or double-click REC on the status bar.

Running a macro

You can run a macro with a keyboard shortcut or from a toolbar or menu if you assigned the macro to a toolbar, menu, or keyboard shortcut. Whether you did that or not, however, you can always run macros from the Macro dialog box:

1. Carefully place the cursor where you want the macro to do its job.

2. Choose <u>T</u>ools⇨<u>M</u>acro. The Macro dialog box opens.

3. Click the appropriate macro in the <u>M</u>acro Name list.

4. Choose the <u>R</u>un button.

Deleting a macro

To delete a macro, choose it in the Macro dialog box and click the <u>D</u>elete button.

Master Documents for Really Big Jobs

For really big jobs like books, create a *master document*. A master document is a collection of subdocuments that make up the book. Master documents make it easier to organize and manage big jobs. Every change you make in a subdocument is made to the master document as well, and changes made to the master document are also made to the subdocument. So all you have to do is go to the master document and collapse or expand the headings to see how your work is progressing.

With a master document, it's easy to promote or demote headings. All you have to do is click buttons on the Master Document toolbar. You can also move text easily in a master document. And when you want to see how your book is organized, all you have to do is change to Master Document view and have a look.

If you just started writing and organizing your opus, creating a master document is easy. It's a bit harder to assemble documents you've already written or are working on and put them in a master document.

Creating a new master document

To create a new master document:

1. Click the New button, press Ctrl+N, or choose File⇨New to open a new document.

2. Choose View⇨Master Document. The Master Document toolbar appears. Many of these tools are the same those on the Outline toolbar.

3. Enter the chapter titles and headings. This is the outline you will use to write your book. As you enter headings and titles, use the Style list to assign heading levels. For example, give the Heading 1 style to chapter titles. Headings and subheadings within chapters are assigned styles Heading 2, Heading 3, and so on.

4. Select the first batch of headings to turn them into a subdocument and click the Create Subdocument button.

5. Keep doing this until you've selected and created all the subdocuments. When you're done, your document looks something like the first figure on the following page. Notice the subdocument icons on the left.

6. Choose File⇨Save As to save the master document and all its subdocuments.

7. Choose a folder to save the file in, type a name for the master document in the File name box, and click the Save button.

Word 95 creates and names the subdocuments as well as the master document. In the second figure on the next page, you can see how the subdocuments in the preceding figure were saved and named.

Now all you have to do is open a subdocument and start working. Every change you make in a subdocument is made to the master document as well. You can also click a subdocument icon in the master document to go straight to the subdocument.

Assembling documents for a master document

Maybe you've already written several documents and want to assemble them into a master document. Follow these instructions:

1. Click the New button, press Ctrl+N, or choose File⇨New to open a new document.

2. Choose View⇨Master Document.

Click to see text formatting

Subdocument icon

Create subdocument

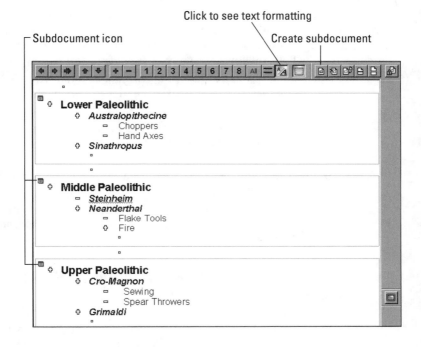

Subdocuments

Master document

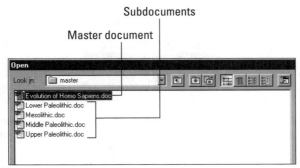

 3. Click the Insert Subdocument button.

4. In the Insert Subdocument dialog box, find and select the first document that you want to include in your master document.

5. Click the Open button. The file is inserted.

6. If styles are different in the subdocument and the master document template, Word 95 asks what to do about it. You can apply the subdocument's styles or use the styles in the master document template by clicking <u>Y</u>es or <u>N</u>o.

7. Click the 1, 2, or 3 button to see only the first one, two, or three levels of headings. That makes it easier to work in Master Document view.

8. Go to the bottom of the master document, click the Insert Subdocument button, and insert another file. Keep doing this until you've inserted all the subdocuments.

9. Choose <u>F</u>ile⇨Save <u>A</u>s to save the master document and all its subdocuments.

10. Choose a folder to save the master document in, type a descriptive name for the master document in the File <u>n</u>ame box, and click the <u>S</u>ave button.

Removing, moving, locking, splitting, merging, and renaming subdocuments

To remove or rearrange subdocuments, open the master document and change to Master Document view by choosing <u>V</u>iew⇨<u>M</u>aster Document or clicking the Master Document button in the lower-left corner of the document window. Click the 1 button to see only the first heading in every subdocument. Then do the following:

✦ **Removing:** Select the subdocument by clicking its subdocument icon. Then click the Remove Subdocument button and press the Delete key. Removing a subdocument this way does not delete the subdocument — it merely removes it from the master document.

✦ **Moving:** Word 95 says that you can move a subdocument by clicking its icon and dragging its icon to a new place, but when I try to do this I only succeed in dropping one subdocument into another. To move a subdocument, I prefer to remove it and then reinsert it.

✦ **Moving a heading:** Click the icon to the left of the heading and drag it to a new location.

✦ **Merging:** To merge two subdocuments and make them a single subdocument, move the subdocuments so that they are next to each other, if necessary. Select the first by clicking its subdocument icon, and select the second by Shift+clicking its icon. You can merge more than one document by Shift+clicking this way. Finally, click the Merge Subdocument button and save the master document.

✦ **Splitting:** To divide a subdocument into two parts and create two subdocuments, select the heading that you want to be the first in the new subdocument. Do this by clicking its icon. Then click the Split Subdocument button.

✦ **Renaming:** To rename a subdocument, you have to do so within the master document. Double-click the subdocument icon to open the subdocument. Choose File➪Save As, type a new name in the File name text box, and click Save. Then close the subdocument.

✦ **Locking:** If you are sharing your master document with others, you can lock subdocuments to keep others from tampering with them. When a subdocument is locked, people can read it but can't change it in any way. To lock a subdocument, click its icon and click the Lock button. You'll see the Lock icon below the subdocument icon. Click the Lock button again to unlock the subdocument.

Outlines for Organizing Your Work

Outline view is a great way to see at a glance how your document is organized and whether you need to organize it differently. To take advantage of this feature, you must have used the Style menu to assign heading levels to the headings in your document. In Outline view, you can see all the headings in your document. If a section is in the wrong place, you can move it simply by dragging an icon or by pressing one of the buttons on the Outline toolbar.

To see a document in Outline view, choose View➪Outline or click the Outline View button in the lower-left corner of the screen. On the following page is a sample document in Outline view with the All button selected to show all the headings and the normal text in paragraphs.

To change how much of a document you see in Outline view:

✦ **Headings:** Click a Show Heading button (1 through 8) to see different heading levels.

✦ **All headings:** Click the All button to see the whole show.

✦ **Headings in one section:** If you want to see the headings and text in only one section of a document, choose that section and click the Expand button. Click the Collapse button when you're done.

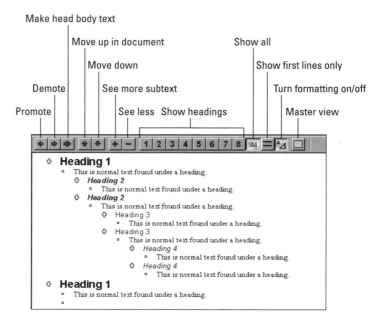

Make head body text

Move up in document

Move down

Show all

Show first lines only

Demote

See more subtext

Turn formatting on/off

Promote

See less   Show headings

Master view

✦ **Normal text:** Click the Show First Line Only button to see only the first line in each paragraph. First lines are followed by an ellipsis (...) so you know that more text follows.

Notice the plus icons and square icons next to the headings and the text. A plus icon means that the heading has subtext under it. For example, headings almost always have plus icons because text comes after them, but body text has a square icon because it is lowest on the Outline totem pole.

To select text in Outline view, click either the plus sign or the square icon. With that done, you can do the following tasks:

✦ **Promote a head:** Click the Promote button to move a heading up the ladder. For example, you can promote a Heading 2 to a Heading 1.

✦ **Demote a head:** Click the Demote button to bust down a Heading 1 to a Heading 2, for example.

✦ **Make a head into normal text:** Click the Demote to Body Text button to make a heading into text.

✦ **Move a section:** To move a section up or down in the document, click the Move Up or Move Down button. You can also drag the plus sign or square icon to a new location.

When you move, promote, or demote a head or section, you do the same to all the subtext beneath it. To select more than one section, Shift+click its icon.

Rearranging the Toolbars

To make it easier to work with toolbars, you can drag them around on-screen. You can remove buttons from the toolbars and replace them with buttons of your own choosing. You can also create your own toolbars and even invent new toolbar buttons.

To find out what a button on a toolbar does, move the mouse pointer over it. A one- or two-word description appears. Look in the status bar for a longer explanation of the button.

Displaying other toolbars

Two toolbars appear at the top of the Word 95 window: the Standard toolbar and the Formatting toolbar. To place new toolbars in the window:

1. Choose View➪Toolbars.

2. Click the names of the toolbars you need.

3. Click OK.

You can also put new toolbars on a window by right-clicking any toolbar and choosing a new toolbar from the shortcut menu. To remove a toolbar, choose it again from the shortcut menu.

You can drag a toolbar into the window and reposition it or change its shape:

✦ To reposition a toolbar, click in the toolbar (but not on a button) and drag it into the window.

✦ To change a toolbar's shape, place the mouse on a border. When you see the two-headed arrow, drag the border until the toolbar is the shape you want.

This figure shows all the toolbars on the Toolbars dialog box. They have been dragged into the window and reshaped:

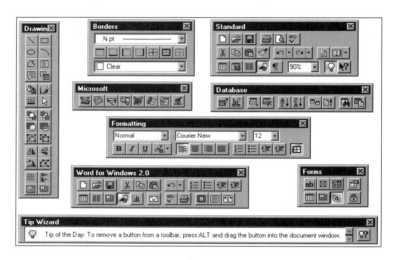

To remove a toolbar you've dragged into the window, click its Close button (the *X* in the upper-right corner). Double-click its title bar to move it back to its rightful place at the top or bottom of the window.

Putting your own buttons on toolbars

For all I know, you never do some of the tasks that the buttons on the Standard and Formatting toolbars were put there to help you do. If you're not using a button, you can take it off the toolbar and replace it with a button you do use. Replacing buttons is easy, and if you make a mistake, it's easy to get the original toolbars back. If you don't have Microsoft Excel, for example, you don't need the Insert Microsoft Excel Worksheet button. And if you don't have an Address Book, you can chuck the Insert Address button and put a button you do use in its place.

To change which buttons appear on toolbars:

1. Put the toolbar whose buttons you want to change on-screen.

2. Choose Tools⬡Customize, or right-click a toolbar and choose Customize from the shortcut menu. The Customize dialog box appears.

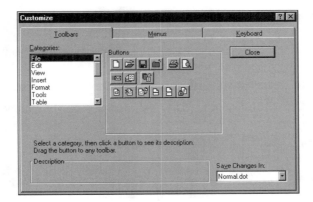

The <u>C</u>ategories list in this dialog box lists all the menus in Word 95 along with the styles, macros, AutoText entries, and fonts that are available in the template you're using. In the Buttons box is a button that corresponds to each menu command. To see what a button does, click it in the dialog box and read the description in the Description box.

3. To remove a button from a toolbar, simply drag it off the toolbar. The button disappears.

To add a button, click in the <u>C</u>ategories box. Find the one you want to add, select the button in the Buttons box, and drag it to the place on the toolbar where you want it to appear.

4. If you want your new toolbar arrangement to appear only in certain templates, click the Sa<u>v</u>e Changes In drop-down menu and choose the template.

5. Click Close.

You can also move buttons between toolbars by dragging them from toolbar to toolbar.

If you make a boo-boo and wish that you hadn't fooled with the buttons on the toolbar:

1. Choose <u>V</u>iew⇨<u>T</u>oolbars.

2. Choose the toolbar name in the <u>T</u>oolbars box.

3. Click the <u>R</u>eset button.

4. Click OK in the Reset Toolbar dialog box.

Creating your own toolbar

You can also create a new toolbar with your favorite buttons on it. If you want, you can even create toolbar buttons for styles, fonts, AutoText entries, and macros.

1. Choose View➪Toolbars to open the Toolbars dialog box.

2. Click the New button. The New Toolbar dialog box appears:

3. Type a name for your toolbar in the Toolbar Name box. The name you type here appears in the Toolbars dialog box.

4. If necessary, choose a template in the Make Toolbar Available To drop-down list.

5. Click OK. The Customize dialog box appears.

6. To add a button, click in the Categories box. When you find the button you want to add, select it in the Buttons box and drag it onto the toolbar. Don't worry — the toolbar will get bigger as you add buttons.

7. Keep adding buttons this way.

8. If you want to add to the toolbar a style, macro, AutoText entry, or font from the template you're using, scroll to the bottom of the Categories list, click the style, macro, AutoText entry, or font, and drag it to the toolbar. The Custom Button dialog box appears:

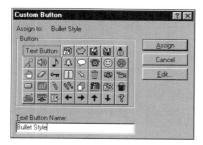

9. Decide what the button should look like:

  • **Symbol:** Click a symbol in the button list and click the Assign button.

- **Text Button:** Click Text Button, type a name in the <u>T</u>ext Button Name box, and click the <u>A</u>ssign button.

- **Customized Symbol:** To create your own symbol, click the <u>E</u>dit button, use the tools in the Button Editor to design the symbol, click OK, and click the <u>A</u>ssign button.

10. Drag the toolbar buttons to get the right spacing on the toolbar. You can also move buttons by dragging them to new places.

11. When you're done creating your new toolbar, click Close in the Customize dialog box.

Here is a toolbar I created myself. Instead of choosing these styles from the Style menu, all I have to do is click a button on this toolbar:

 You can always delete a toolbar you made yourself. Choose <u>V</u>iew⇨<u>T</u>oolbars, select the toolbar in the Toolbars dialog box, and click <u>D</u>elete. Click <u>Y</u>es when you're asked whether you really want to delete it.

Repeating an Action — and Quicker This Time

 The <u>E</u>dit menu has a command called <u>R</u>epeat that you can choose to repeat your last action, and it can be a mighty time-saver. The command changes names, depending on what you did last.

For example, if you just changed a heading style, the command is called <u>E</u>dit⇨Repeat <u>S</u>tyle. To change another heading in the same way, move the cursor to the heading and choose <u>E</u>dit⇨Repeat <u>S</u>tyle (or press F4 or Ctrl+Y) instead of going to the trouble of clicking the Style menu and choosing a heading style from the drop-down list.

If you had to type "I will not talk in class" 100 times, all you would have to do is write it once and choose <u>E</u>dit⇨<u>R</u>epeat Typing (or press F4 or Ctrl+Y) 99 times.

Similar to the <u>E</u>dit⇨<u>R</u>epeat command is the Redo button. It "redoes" the commands you "undid" with the Undo menu or Undo button. If you've "undone" a bunch of commands and regret having done so, pull down the Redo menu by clicking its down arrow and choose the commands you thoughtlessly "undid" the first time around.

See "Undoing a Mistake" in Part II to find another quick way to enter text and formats.

Searching with Wildcards

When you can't find a file or are searching for a word in a document, wildcards can come in handy. A *wildcard* is a single character or group of characters that represent characters in a file name or word. This table lists common wildcards and explains how to use them.

Wildcard	How to Use It
?	Represents a single character. Entering **Peter?.doc** in a Find File dialog box finds files named *Peter1.doc* and *Peter2.doc,* but not *Peter10.doc.*
*	Represents a group of characters or a single character. Entering **Peter*.doc** finds *Peter1.doc* as well as *Peter10.doc.*
[xx]	Represents specific characters to search for, where *xx* are the characters. Entering **P[ae]ter.doc** finds files named *Pater.doc* and *Peter.doc,* but not *Piter.doc* or *Puter.doc.*
[!x]	Represents a character you *don't* want to find, where *x* is the character. Entering **P[!e]ter.doc** finds *Pater.doc, Piter.doc,* and *Puter.doc,* but not *Peter.doc.*
[x-z]	Represents a group of consecutive characters, where *x* and *z* are the characters. Entering **P[b-d]ter.doc** finds *Pbter.doc, Pcter.doc,* and *Pdter.doc,* but not *Pater.doc* or *Peter.doc.*

Desktop Publishing

Once upon a time, word processors were nothing more than glorified typewriters. They were good for typing and basic formatting, but not much else. Over the years, however, Microsoft Word and other word processors have become desktop publishing programs in their own right.

Part VI explains advanced formatting techniques in Word 95. If you're in charge of the company newsletter, or you just want to impress your impressionable friends, check out the entries in this part.

In this part...

- ✔ **Keeping text and graphics in the same place**
- ✔ **Putting borders and shading on paragraphs and graphics**
- ✔ **Changing the color of text**
- ✔ **Creating, editing, and formatting tables**
- ✔ **Drawing in Word**
- ✔ **Using frames to help position text and graphics**
- ✔ **Creating "landscape" documents**
- ✔ **Importing clip art into a document**

Anchoring Text and Graphics

Suppose you want a paragraph or a graphic to stay in the same place. Normally, what is in the middle of page 1 is pushed to the bottom of the page or to page 2 when you insert paragraphs at the start of a document. What if you want the paragraph or graphic to say put, come hell or high water?

In that case, you can *anchor* it in one place. After you drop anchor, text flows around your graphic or paragraph, and your graphic or paragraph stays put.

To anchor a paragraph, graphic, table, or figure to the page so that it never moves:

1. Choose Insert⇨Frame and draw a frame around the item in question. (*See* "Inserting a Frame for Text or a Graphic" later in this part if you need help inserting a frame or positioning it on the page.)

2. Format the text or graphic. You can shade the box and draw a border around it if you want (*see* "Bordering and Shading Paragraphs and Graphics" later in this part).

3. Click inside the frame and choose Format⇨Frame. The Frame dialog box appears:

Click to drop anchor

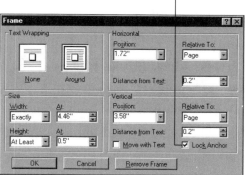

4. Choose None or Around, depending on how you want text to flow beside your paragraph or graphic.

5. In the Horizontal area, enter a position of your own or choose a Position option, if necessary, and choose Page from the Relative To drop-down menu.

6. In the Distance from Te_x_t box, click to tell Word 95 how close text can come to the top and bottom of the frame.

7. In the Vertical area, enter a position of your own or choose a Position option if you need to and choose Page from the R_e_lative To menu.

8. In the Distance _f_rom Text box, tell Word 95 how close text can come to the sides of the frame if text is going to wrap around the sides.

9. Remove the check mark from the _M_ove with Text check box.

10. Click the Loc_k_ Anchor check box.

11. Click OK.

The following figure shows an example of an anchored paragraph. No matter how much news goes before this anchored frame, this important notice stays smack-dab in the middle of page 1:

We will be holding a potluck dinner on Saturday, May 12 at 6:00 to celebrate the end of the fishing season. Bring your favorite dish and something to drink. Family and friends are welcome too.

 Due to the unfortunate incident in Sag Harbor last month, all pilots are reminded to anchor their boats in port...

Our softball team completed a less than glorious season with a glorious win over the Great Neck Mighty Swans last Saturday afternoon. We won, believe it or not, and upped our record to 1 win, 9 losses. Way to go, Moby Dicks!

Bordering and Shading Paragraphs and Graphics

 By placing borders around text or a graphic and shading the area inside the borders, you can brighten up a page considerably. Here is an example of an announcement that has been shaded and given a three-dimensional "shadow" border:

The building manager and the fire department will conduct a test of the fire alarms in the building on Tuesday, December 11 at 10:00. Ignore the fire alarms—unless, of course, there is a real fire.

The fastest way to get borders and shading is to create a frame and use the Borders toolbar:

1. Create a frame around the paragraph, table, or graphic (*see* "Inserting a Frame for Text or a Graphic" later in this part).

2. Click the perimeter of the frame to select it.

3. Click the Borders button or right-click a toolbar and choose Borders from the shortcut menu to display the Borders toolbar.

4. Click the down arrow on the Line Style menu and choose a line.

5. Click the Outside Border button.

6. Choose a shading from the Shading menu.

The other way to create borders and shading is to use the Format➪Borders and Shading command. This way, you get a few extra options:

1. Select the paragraph to which you want to add borders and shading. To apply borders to a table, select it. If you're putting borders and shading on a graphic, you have to put the graphic in a frame first (*see* "Inserting a Frame for Text or a Graphic" later in this part).

2. Choose Format➪Borders and Shading. The Borders tab of the Paragraph Borders and Shading dialog box appears:

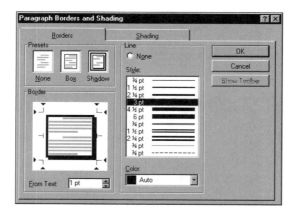

3. Choose a Presets option:

• None removes the border.

• Box creates a simple box.

• Shadow creates a three-dimensional "shadow" border.

4. Choose a line from the St<u>y</u>le menu to create the border.

5. Wrestle with the Bo<u>r</u>der box to create borders of different widths and get the borders just right. To choose a side, click it. Then choose a line from the St<u>y</u>le menu. Click a border line again to remove it. If worse comes to worst, click the <u>N</u>one option button and start all over.

6. In the <u>F</u>rom Text box, click the up arrow to tell Word 95 how close text can come to the border.

7. If you want a color for your border, choose one from the <u>C</u>olor menu.

8. Click the <u>S</u>hading tab to get at the shading options:

Watch this box

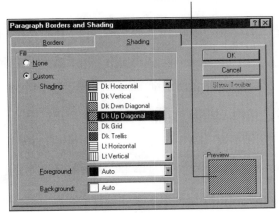

9. Click the <u>C</u>ustom option button to create a shading.

10. Choose a shade from the Sha<u>d</u>ing menu and keep your eyes on the Preview box to see what your choice looks like.

11. If you will be printing on a color printer, you can choose colors for the shading in the <u>F</u>oreground and B<u>a</u>ckground boxes. Foreground colors pertain to the dots, lines, and stripes in the foreground of a pattern. Background colors appear behind the dots, lines, and stripes.

12. Click OK.

Coloring Text

If you're lucky enough to own or have access to a color printer, you can print text in different colors. And even if you don't own a color printer, you can change the color of text on-screen. You might do that to call attention to parts of a document, for example. Word 95 offers 14 colors, plus white and black. To change the color of text:

1. Select the text.

2. Choose Format⇨Font. The Font dialog box appears:

Click to choose a color

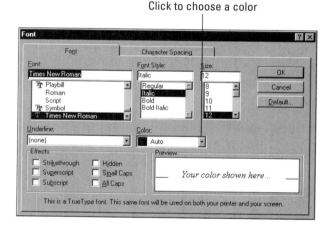

3. Click the down arrow in the Color menu and choose a color. Look in the Preview box to see what each color looks like.

4. Click OK.

To remove colors:

1. Either select the entire document (by choosing Edit⇨Select All or pressing Ctrl+A) or select the text from which you want to remove colors.

2. Choose Format⇨Font.

3. Click the Color drop-down menu.

4. Choose Auto.

Constructing the Perfect Table

As everyone who has ever worked on one knows, tables are a chore. Getting all the columns to fit, making columns and rows the right width and height, and editing the text in a table is not easy. So problematic are tables that Word 95 has devoted an entire menu to constructing them: the T<u>a</u>ble menu. Fortunately for you, the commands on this menu make formatting and working with tables easy.

This section explains how to create tables, enter text into tables, change the number and size of columns and rows, and format tables.

Like so much else in Computerland, tables have their own jargon. A *cell,* for example, is the box that is formed where a row and column intersect. Each cell holds one data item. The *header row* is the name of the labels along the top row that explain what is in the columns below. *Borders* are the lines in the table. The *gridlines* are the dotted lines that show where the columns and rows are. Gridlines do not print — they are there to help you format your table. Only the borders print when you print a table.

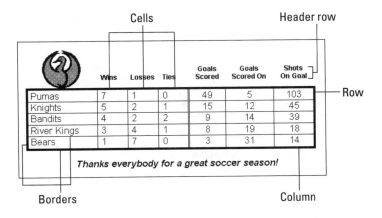

	Wins	Losses	Ties	Goals Scored	Goals Scored On	Shots On Goal
Pumas	7	1	0	49	5	103
Knights	5	2	1	15	12	45
Bandits	4	2	2	9	14	39
River Kings	3	4	1	8	19	18
Bears	1	7	0	3	31	14

Thanks everybody for a great soccer season!

Sometimes a table is not the best way to present information. If you find yourself wrestling with a table to make all the data fit inside it, you likely made the wrong choice for presenting your data. Try converting the table into text (with the T<u>a</u>ble⇨Con<u>v</u>ert Table to Text command) and using bulleted lists or headings and paragraphs instead of a table.

Creating a table

There are three ways to create the cells and rows for a table. You can click the Insert Table button, choose the Table⇨Insert Table command, or convert text you've already entered into a table.

The fastest way to create a table is to click the Insert Table button on the Standard toolbar:

1. Place the cursor where you want the table to go.

2. Click the Insert Table button. A menu showing a table with four rows and five columns appears.

3. Click to say how many columns and rows you want. For example, if you click where the cursor is in the preceding illustration, you get a table with three rows and four columns.

The Insert Table button works fine for simple tables, but what if you want a larger table? In that case, use the Table⇨Insert Table command:

1. Place the cursor where you want the table to be.

2. Choose Table⇨Insert Table. The Insert Table dialog box appears:

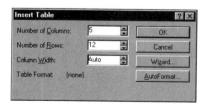

3. In the Number of Columns box, enter the number of columns you want.

4. In the Number of Rows box, enter the number of rows you want.

5. Word 95 gives columns a uniform width based on how many columns are in the table, but you can change the width of all columns in the table by clicking the arrows in the Column Width box.

6. If you want extra help with your table, click one of these buttons:

- **Wizard:** Opens the Table Wizard so that Word 95 can help you construct the table in step-by-step fashion.

- **AutoFormat:** Opens a dialog box from which you can choose one of Word 95's table formats. These formats are explained in the section, "Formatting a table."

7. Click OK.

The third way to create a table is to convert text that you've already entered. Going this route is risky, however, because Word 95 has trouble dividing plain text into rows and columns. If you want to try it, follow these steps:

1. Place a comma or a tab in the text where you want columns to be divided.

2. Enter a paragraph break where you want each row to end.

3. Select the text you want to include in the table.

4. Choose Table➪Convert Text to Table.

5. Choose the number of columns and rows you want in the Convert Text to Table dialog box.

6. Tell Word 95 how you separated columns in step 1 (with commas or tabs).

7. Click OK.

Entering text in a table

After you create the table and can see the gridlines (the dotted lines that divide the rows and columns), you can start entering text. (If you don't see the gridlines, choose Table➪Gridlines.) All you have to do is click in a cell and start typing. To help you work more quickly, here are some shortcuts for moving the cursor in a table:

Press	*Moves the Cursor to*
Tab	Next column in row
Shift+Tab	Previous column in row
Alt+Home	Start of row
Alt+End	End of row
↓	Row below
↑	Row above
Alt+Page Up	Top of column
Alt+Page Down	Bottom of column

If you need to add a row at the bottom of the table to enter more text, place the cursor in the last column of the last row and press the Tab key.

Changing the layout of a table

Very likely, you created too many or too few rows or columns for your table. Some columns are probably too wide, and others may be too narrow. If that is the case, you have to change the layout of the table by deleting, inserting, and changing the size of columns and rows. (Putting borders around tables and embellishing them in other ways are explained in the next section, "Formatting a table.")

This section explains

✦ Selecting rows, columns, and an entire table

✦ Inserting and deleting columns and rows

✦ Rearranging columns and rows

✦ Resizing columns and rows

A special Word 95 feature makes text fit on the computer screen no matter how far it strays into the right margin in real life. This feature is nice when you're working with documents, but it makes things very confusing when you're working with tables and have to see exactly how wide columns are and whether they fit across the page. Be sure to turn off this feature if it's on. To do that:

1. Choose Tools➪Options.

2. Click the View tab.

3. Click in the Wrap to Window check box to remove the check mark if there is a check mark in it.

Before you can fool with cells, rows, or columns, you have to select them:

✦ **Cells:** To select a cell, move the cursor over it. When the cursor changes into a pointer arrow, click once. You can select several cells at once by dragging the cursor over them.

✦ **Rows:** Place the cursor in the left margin and click to select one row, or click and drag to select several. You can also select rows by placing the cursor in the row you want to select and then choosing the Table➪Select Row command. To select several rows, select cells in the rows and then choose Table➪Select Row.

↓ ✦ **Columns:** To select a column, move the cursor to the top of the column. When the cursor changes into a fat down-pointing arrow (at left), click once. You can click and drag to select several columns. The other way to select a column is to click anywhere in the column and choose Table⇨Select Column. To select several columns with this command, select cells in the columns and then choose Table⇨Select Column.

✦ **A table:** To select a table, click in the table and choose Table⇨Select Table or press Alt+5. (Press the 5 on the numeric keypad, not the one on the keyboard, and make sure that Num Lock is turned off.)

Here's the lowdown on inserting and deleting columns and rows:

✦ **Inserting columns:** To insert a blank column, select the column to the right of where you want the new column to go. If you want to insert two or more columns, select the number of columns you want to add. Then choose Table⇨Insert Columns, right-click in the selection, and choose Insert Columns from the shortcut menu, or simply press the Insert Table button on the Standard toolbar (now it's called Insert Columns).

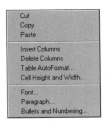

✦ **Deleting columns:** To delete columns, select them. Then either choose Table⇨Delete Columns or right-click the selection and choose Delete Columns.

✦ **Inserting rows:** To insert a blank row, select the row below which you want the new one to appear. If you want to insert more than one row, select more than one. Then choose Table⇨Insert Rows, right-click in the selection, and choose Insert Rows from the shortcut menu, or just press the Insert Table button on the toolbar (it's called Insert Rows now). You can also insert a row at the end of a table by moving the cursor into the last cell in the last row and pressing Tab.

✦ **Deleting rows:** To delete rows, select them and choose Table⇨Delete Rows or else right-click and choose Delete Rows from the shortcut menu.

Because there is no elegant way to move a column or row, you should move only one at a time. If you try to move several at once, you open a can of worms that is best left unopened. To move a column or row:

1. Select the column or row you want to move.

2. Right-click in the selection and choose Cut from the shortcut menu. The column or row disappears to the Clipboard.

3. Move the column or row:

- **Column:** Move the cursor across the top of the columns and slide it delicately to the spot between two existing columns to which you want to move the column. When the cursor turns into a fat down-pointing arrow, right-click and choose Paste Columns from the shortcut menu.

- **Row:** Move the cursor into the first column of the row above which you want to move your row. In other words, if you're placing the row between what are now rows 6 and 7, put the cursor in row 7. Then right-click and choose Paste Rows from the shortcut menu.

The fastest way to rearrange the rows in a table is to use the Table⇨Sort command, which rearranges all the rows on the basis of data in one column. Rearranging a table this way is called *sorting*. For example, the first soccer standings table shown here is arranged, or sorted, on the "Wins" column, in descending order from the most wins to the fewest. The second table is sorted alphabetically on the team name column in ascending order. The same data is in both tables, but the rows have been arranged in different ways.

	Wins	Losses	Ties	Goals Scored	Goals Scored On	Shots On Goal
Pumas	7	1	0	49	5	103
Knights	5	2	1	15	12	45
Bandits	4	2	2	9	14	39
River Kings	3	4	1	8	19	18
Bears	1	7	0	3	31	14

Bandits	4	2	2	9	14	39
Bears	1	7	0	3	31	14
Knights	5	2	1	15	12	45
Pumas	7	1	0	49	5	103
River Kings	3	4	1	8	19	18

When you rearrange a table this way, the formatting gets rearranged as well as the data. You likely have to go back into the table and reformat everything.

To sort the rows in a table:

1. Click in the table.

2. Choose Table⇨Sort. The Sort dialog box appears:

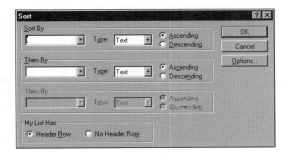

3. In the Sort By drop-down list, choose which column to sort the table by.

4. In the Type box, choose Text, Number, or Date to tell Word 95 what kind of data is in the column you chose in step 1.

5. Click the Ascending or Descending option button.

- Ascending arranges text from A to Z, numbers from smallest to largest, and dates from the oldest in time to the most recent.

- Descending arranges text from Z to A, numbers from largest to smallest, and dates from most recent to oldest.

6. The Then By boxes tell Word 95 how to sort the table in the event of a tie. For example, if you are sorting on a last name column and there are two Smiths in the table, Word 95 needs to know which Smith should come first. In this case, you would choose the first name column (whatever number it happens to be) in the Then By box, choose Text in the Type box, and click Ascending to put Andre Smith before Salvador Smith in the new, rearranged table.

7. If your table has a header row, the Header Row option button should already be selected to keep the column labels from getting mixed into the sort. If your table doesn't have a header row, No Header Row should be selected, because you want the first row to be rearranged, too. Make sure that these option buttons are chosen correctly.

8. Click OK.

By far, the easiest way to change the width of columns and the height of rows is to "eyeball it." To make a column wider or narrower, simply move the cursor onto a gridline. When the cursor changes into what looks like a German cross, start dragging. You can also slide the column bars on the ruler (if you're in Page Layout view) to change the width of columns. Tug and pull, tug and pull until the columns look just right.

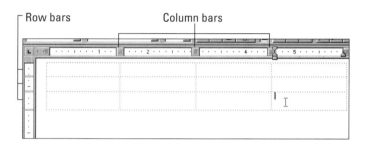

Word 95 adjusts the height of rows to accommodate text, but you can change row heights yourself by dragging the row bars on the vertical ruler (in Page Layout view).

The other technique for adjusting row heights and column widths is to use the Table⇨Cell Height and Width command and blindly try your luck with the settings in the Cell Height and Width dialog box. This technique isn't nearly as useful as "eyeballing it," however, because the dialog box doesn't have a Preview screen and you can't see what your choices do to the table.

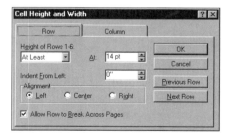

The Row tab in the Cell Height and Width dialog box is useful for fixing rows that are packed in too tightly. To provide more space between rows:

1. Click in the table or, if you want to adjust a few rows, select them.

2. Choose Table⇨Cell Height and Width.

3. In the Height of Rows menu, choose At Least to make sure that there is a certain minimum amount of space between rows. If you want all the rows to be the exact same height, choose Exactly. At minimum, rows should be at least 2 points higher than the font you're using. For example, if your letters are 12 points high, your rows should be 14 points high.

4. In the At box, click the arrows to adjust the height of rows. If you chose At Least in step 3, a number already appears in the box. Click the up arrow to add more space between rows.

5. Click OK.

The Column tab of the Cell Height and Width dialog box has one useful button called AutoFit. Click it if you've pulled and tugged your columns all out of proportion and want Word 95 to resize columns so that they all fit evenly on the page.

Formatting a table

After you enter the text, put the rows and columns in place, and make them the right size, the fun begins. Now you can dress up your table and make it look snazzy.

Almost everything you can do to a document you can do to a table by selecting parts of it and choosing menu commands or clicking buttons. You can change text fonts, align data in the cells, and even import a graphic into a cell. You can also play with the borders that divide the rows and columns and "shade" columns, rows, and cells by filling them with gray shades or a black background.

The fastest way to get a good-looking table is to let Word 95 do the work for you:

1. Click your table.

2. Choose Table⇨AutoFormat or right-click in the table and choose Table AutoFormat. The Table AutoFormat dialog box appears.

3. Rummage through the Formats menu until you find a table to your liking. You can see what tables look like in the Preview box.

4. Check and uncheck the Formats to Apply and Apply Special Formats To check boxes. As you do so, watch the Preview box to see what your choices do.

5. When you have the right table format, click OK.

Watch this box!

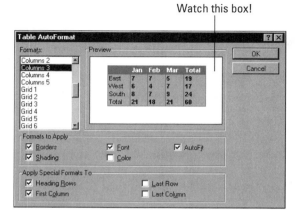

Drawing the borders

Drawing the borders that divide rows and columns and surround the table itself is easier than you might think. Word 95 has a special toolbar for doing just that:

1. Click the Borders button or right-click a toolbar and choose Borders to display the Borders toolbar.

Line Style menu   Border buttons   Shading menu

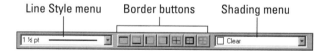

2. Select the part of the table to which you want to apply the border. For example, to put a border on the left side of a cell, select the cell; along the top or bottom of a row, select the row; along the side of a column, select the column; or around the entire table, select it.

3. Click the down-pointing arrow beside the Line Style menu and choose a line width or double line. Choose None or click the No Border button if you don't want a border or you are removing one that is already there.

4. Click one of the seven Border buttons in the middle of the toolbar to apply the border. For example, to put a border along the top of a row you've selected, click the Top Border button.

5. Apply borders to other parts of the table that you select in step 2:

- **Same border:** To apply a border of the same line style to another side of the part of the table that you select in step 2, simply click another button. For example, to apply the same border along the bottom of a row as you did to the top, click the Bottom Border button.

- **Different border:** To apply a different border to another side of the part of the table, click the Line Style menu and choose a new line style. Then click a different Border button.

6. Select a different part of the table and repeat steps 3 through 5.

Making the borders look good requires some experimentation. Very likely, you want most of the cells on the inside of the table to have the same border. In that case, select those cells, choose a line style, and click the Inside Border button. To make the outside border of a table a uniform style, select the table, choose a line style, and click the Outside Border button.

Shading parts of a table

Shading and black backgrounds call readers' attention to the important parts of a table. Usually, shading is used in the header row and in a summary row — for example, in the "totals" column or in the bottom row. In this table, the header row has a black background, the highest production figure in each category is shaded at 20 percent gray, and the summary column at the bottom is shaded at 40 percent gray:

Production Plant	Bubble Gum (tons)	Candy Canes (units)	Cotton Candy (acres)	Licorice (sticks)	Lollipops (units)
Boca Raton, FL	119	46,223	918	511,112	290,412
Peoria, IL	335	39,918	456	37,801	871,932
Poughkeepsie, NY	211	118,561	712	567,912	317,206
Waukegan, IL	56	99,987	498	998,912	298,118
Totals	721	304,689	2,584	2,115,737	1,777,668

To "shade" or give a solid black background to a part of a table:

1. If it's not already on-screen, click the Borders button or right-click a toolbar and choose Borders to display the Borders toolbar.

2. Select the part of the table that you want to shade.

3. Click the down-pointing arrow on the Shading menu and choose an option. Choose Clear to remove shading or Solid (100%) to get a black background.

Repeating header rows on subsequent pages

Making sure that the header row appears on a new page if the table breaks across pages is absolutely essential. Without a header row, readers can't tell what the information in a table is or means. To make the header row (or rows) repeat, place the cursor in the header row (or select the header rows if you have more than one) and choose Table⇨Headings.

Merging and splitting cells and tables

The cells in the first header row of the following table have been merged to create "supercategories." Instead of eight cells, the first row has only four:

West		Midwest		South		East	
California	Washington	Illinois	Nebraska	Georgia	Louisiana	Massachusetts	New York

To merge cells in a table:

1. Select the cells you want to merge.

2. Choose Table⇨Merge Cells.

In the same vein, you can split a cell into two or more cells:

1. Click in the cell you want to split.

2. Choose Table⇨Split Cells.

3. In the Split Cells dialog box, declare how many cells you want to split the cell into and click OK.

Still in the same vein, you can split a table as well:

1. Place the cursor in what you want to be the first row of the new table.

2. Choose Table⇨Split Table.

Using math formulas in tables

No, you don't have to add the figures in columns and rows yourself; Word 95 gladly does that for you. Word 95 can perform other mathematical calculations as well. To do arithmetic on the figures in a row or column:

1. Put the cursor in the cell that will hold the sum or product of the cells above, below, to the right, or to the left.

2. Choose Table⇨Formula. The Formula dialog box appears:

Units Sold	Total Sale ($)
13	178.12
15	179.33
93	178.00
31	671.13
24	411.12
9	69.13
11	79.40
196	

Formula

Formula:
=SUM(ABOVE)

OK   Cancel

Number Format:

Paste Function: Paste Bookmark:

3. In its wisdom, Word 95 makes a very educated guess about what you want to the formula to do and places a formula in the Formula box. If this isn't the formula you want, click the down-pointing arrow in the Paste F<u>u</u>nction box and choose another formula.

4. In the <u>N</u>umber Format box, click the down-pointing arrow and choose a format for your number.

5. Click OK.

Word 95 does not calculate blank cells in formulas. Enter a **0** in blank cells if you want to include them in calculations.

Drawing in Word 95

Drawing pictures in Word 95 is not for everyone; it's not easy, and getting comfortable with the drawing tools takes a long while. The Drawing toolbar is really a computer program unto itself. You can use it, however, to decorate newsletters, invitations, and notices with shapes and crude drawings.

To make a drawing, click the Drawing button on the Standard toolbar or right-click a toolbar and choose Drawing from the shortcut menu. Simply start drawing on-screen or insert a frame to create a place for your drawing (click the Insert Frame button, the farthest right button on the Drawing toolbar, to insert a frame).

To choose a tool, click it. The mouse changes into a small cross. Drag the mouse to draw a line or create a shape. By tugging and pulling at the selection handles (the black squares at the corners and sides of objects), you can change the shape and size of the objects you draw. You can also drag shapes to new places on-screen.

See also "Inserting Pictures and Graphics in Documents," later in this part, to find out how the Drawing toolbar can help you place text on the pictures you create.

Fixing Spacing Problems in Headings

When you enlarge text for a heading, one or two letters may end up being too close together or too far apart. For example, in the following heading, the *r* and the *n* in *Born* are too close together and almost look like an *m,* and the *T* and *w* in *Twins* are too far apart:

Adjusting the space between two letters is called *kerning,* and it is easy to do in Word 95:

T wins Born to Mrs. Lin

---

1. Select the two letters that are too far apart or too close together.

2. Choose Format⇨Font.

3. Click the Character Spacing tab.

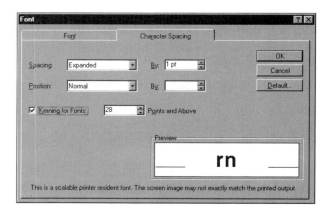

4. In the Spacing menu, choose Expanded to spread the letters out or Condensed to pack them in.

5. Word 95 changes the number in the By box for you, but you can do yet more packing or spreading by clicking the down or up arrow yourself.

6. Click the Kerning for Fonts check box and enter a point size in the Points and Above box if you want Word 95 to kern fonts above a certain point size automatically.

7. Click OK.

Inserting a Frame for Text or a Graphic

Place text or a graphic in a frame when you want to make it stand out on a page. After the frame is in place, you can format it with borders or shading. Frames also make it easy to change the position and size of a graphic. You can make text wrap around them, which makes for a very elegant effect.

The hoi polloi have a real treat this month, as trumpeter **Jimmy Vega** brings his **Swinging Latin All Stars** to Stacey's on Saturday, May 25. "It's been a long time since I've played Muncie," Jimmy reminisced during a recent phone call from Las Vegas, where he and the band have been holed up at the MGM's Plush Room. "I'm really looking forward to it." The band, by all accounts, is *hot, hot, hot*—and Jimmy's chops are better than ever.

On the home front, local yokels **The Swinging Johnsons** and **Dicky Do and the Don'ts** will be holding down the fort at Slim's on the weekend of June 1 and 2. Don't miss this dance party!

♥ ♥ ♥ ♥

Inserting the frame

To insert a frame:

1. Place the cursor roughly where you want the northwest corner of the frame to be.

2. Choose Insert⇨Frame. The cursor changes into a cross. (If you're in Normal view, Word 95 informs you that you should be in Page Layout view and asks whether you want to change views. Click Yes to switch to Page Layout view.)

3. Drag the cross in a southeastern direction to draw the frame. As you drag, dotted lines appear to show its perimeters.

4. Let up on the mouse button.

5. Type text in the frame or choose Insert⇨Picture to import a graphic (*see* "Inserting Pictures and Graphics in Documents," the next section in this part, to see how). The frame grows longer to accommodate text, if necessary. You can format the text and even use the ruler to set tab stops and paragraph indents.

You can also put a frame around text or a graphic that is already on-screen. To do that, select the graphic or text and choose Insert⇨Frame.

Changing and moving the frame

 After the frame is in place, you likely will have to change its size or shape or move it. To do that, select the frame by moving the mouse cursor onto the perimeter. When four arrows appear beneath the mouse cursor, click once. Hatch marks appear around the frame, and black *selection handles* show up on the four corners and four sides.

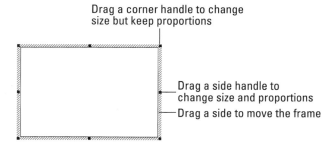

Drag a corner handle to change size but keep proportions

Drag a side handle to change size and proportions

Drag a side to move the frame

 To move a graphic or change its shape or size:

✦ **Moving:** Put the cursor on the perimeter of the frame, but not on one of the selection handles. When four arrows appear beneath the cursor, click and start dragging. Dotted lines show where you are moving the frame. When it's in the right position, release the mouse button.

✦ **Changing size but not proportions:** To change the size of a frame but keep its proportions, move the cursor to one of the selection handles on the corners. The cursor changes into a double-headed arrow. Click and start dragging. Dotted lines show how you are changing the size of the frame. When it's the right size, release the mouse button.

✦ **Changing size and proportions:** To change both the size of the frame *and* its proportions, move the cursor to a selection handle on the side of the frame. When the cursor changes into a double-headed arrow, click and start dragging. Dotted lines show how the frame is being changed. When it is the size and shape you want, release the mouse button.

The following illustration shows the same graphic in three different frames. The original graphic is on the left. For the middle graphic, I pulled a corner selection handle to enlarge the frame but kept the proportions. For the one on the right, I pulled a selection handle on the side to enlarge the frame and change the proportions.

You can also establish the size and shape of a frame with the Frame dialog box. If you go this route, you can't see precisely what your choices do on-screen, but the dialog box offers a few important amenities that are worth knowing about:

1. Click inside the frame and choose Format⇨Frame to see the Frame dialog box. (If you're working with a text frame, you can also double-click the border to get to this dialog box.)

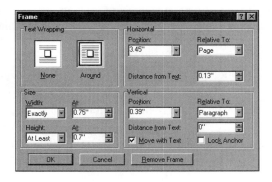

2. Choose None in the Text Wrapping area if you don't want text to wrap around your frame. Otherwise, leave the Around setting as is. In order for Word 95 to wrap text around a frame, there must be at least 1 inch between the side of the frame and the margin or column.

3. In the Size area, choose a <u>W</u>idth option for the frame:

- **Exactly:** Makes the width exactly what you enter in the <u>A</u>t box.

- **Auto:** Lets the width of the frame change to accommodate what's inside it. With this option, Word 95 establishes the width, so you don't enter anything in the <u>A</u>t box.

4. Choose a Height option for the frame in the Size area:

- **Exactly:** Makes the width exactly what you enter in the A<u>t</u> box.

- **Auto:** Lets Word 95 change the height of the frame to accommodate what's inside it.

- **At Least:** Establishes a minimum height. No matter what goes into the frame, it cannot shrink below the height you enter in the A<u>t</u> box.

5. In the Horizontal area, choose the Re<u>l</u>ative To option that describes how the side-to-side measurement for the frame's position should be made. The options are Margin, Page, and Column. For example, to place the frame a certain distance from the left margin, choose Margin. To place it a certain distance from the boundary of the page, choose Page.

6. In the Po<u>s</u>ition box in the Horizontal area, either enter a number that describes a distance or choose Left, Right, Center, Inside, or Outside. If you choose Margin in step 5 and Center here, for example, the frame is centered between the margins.

- The Left option left-aligns the frame with the margin, page, or side of the column.

- The Inside and Outside options are for double-sided, bound pages.

- Outside places the frame farthest from the binding; Inside places it on the inside margin next to the binding.

7. In the Distance from Te<u>x</u>t box, enter a measurement that describes how close text can come to the top and bottom of the frame if you don't care for Word 95's suggestion.

8. In the Vertical area, choose the R<u>e</u>lative To option that describes how to make the top-to-bottom measurement for the frame's position. You can measure from the top of the paragraph, the top margin, or the top of the page.

9. The Po<u>s</u>ition options in the Vertical area are Top, Bottom, Center, or a distance measurement you enter yourself. Either enter a measurement or choose one of the options.

10. In the Distance from Text box, tell Word 95 how close text can come to the left and right sides of the frame — if you don't like Word 95's suggestion.

11. Leave the check mark in the Move with Text check box if you want your frame to move with the page, margin, or paragraph it's attached to when the page, margin, or paragraph moves in your document.

Choose Lock Anchor, however, if you want your frame to stay in the same position. You might choose this option to put a reminder notice in the middle of a page and keep it there no matter how many insertions or deletions you make in your document.

12. Click OK.

To remove a frame (and the text or graphic inside it), select it and press the Delete key. Or else open the Frame dialog box and click the Remove Frame button.

Be careful when you include large frames in a document. A frame does not break across pages, and if it doesn't fit at the bottom of one page, Word 95 moves it to the next. This can cause ugly blank spaces to appear at the bottom of pages.

Inserting Pictures and Graphics in Documents

If you have clip art on your computer, or if you installed one of Microsoft's clip art libraries when you installed Microsoft Office, you have a golden opportunity to embellish your documents with art created by genuine artists. You don't have to tell anyone where this art came from, either. If anybody asks where you got it, wink and say that a "little birdie" gave it to you.

You can insert clip art directly into a document, but it's best to insert it in a frame. That way, you can move it around easily or change its size or shape (*see* "Inserting a Frame for Text or a Graphic," earlier in this part). After you insert the frame, follow these steps:

1. Choose Insert⇨Picture. The Insert Picture dialog box appears.

2. Find the clip art file you want to open. If you installed the Clipart folder as part of Microsoft Office, the dialog box opens to the Clipart folder. You can preview files by clicking them and looking in the box on the right side of the screen.

3. When you find the file you want, click it.

4. Click OK to insert the file in your document.

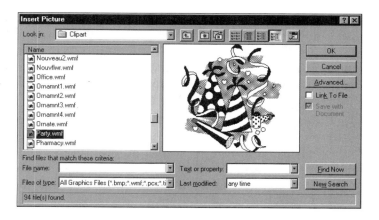

Putting text inside a graphic

It's even possible to include text inside a graphic; but to make it work, you have to import a light-colored graphic and make the box in which the text goes very dark or import a dark graphic and use a light text box. To include text in a graphic:

1. Click the Drawing button or right-click a toolbar and choose Drawing from the shortcut menu. The Drawing toolbar appears.

2. Click the Create Picture button. A special drawing window opens. In this window is a toolbar with two buttons called Reset Picture Boundary and Close Picture.

3. Click the Reset Picture Boundary button, if necessary, and make the boundaries of the picture larger or smaller. As you create your picture, you can't draw outside the boundary. If you do, what strays outside the boundary is cut from your picture when it goes from the drawing window back to your document.

4. Click the Insert Frame button and insert a frame inside the drawing.

5. Follow steps 1 through 4 in the set of instructions given earlier for inserting a graphic into a frame.

6. After you've inserted your graphic, click the Text box button and draw a text frame on the graphic itself.

7. Enter and format text in the box. For example, you can boldface or center it. You can also click the Borders button and add a border, shading, or both to the text box.

8. Adjust the text box so that it is the right size.

9. Click the Close Picture button.

Cropping a graphic

You can *crop* — that is, cut off parts of — a graphic, but not very elegantly. To do that:

1. Click the graphic to make the selection handles appear.

2. Hold down the Shift key and move the mouse pointer over a selection handle. The pointer turns into what looks like a stingray.

3. Drag the mouse into the drawing. Dotted lines appear. What is in the dotted lines is what will be left of the drawing when you release the mouse button.

4. When you've cut off a satisfactory amount, release the mouse button.

Keeping Paragraphs and Lines Together

Where pages break in a document matters a lot. If a figure is on one page and its caption is on the next, or a heading falls at the very bottom of a page and doesn't have any text underneath it, or a chapter title appears at the bottom of a page, you have what Word 95 calls a "text flow" problem. You can prevent these problems with the four check boxes in the Pagination area of the Paragraph dialog box:

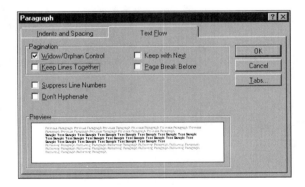

To make sure that a chapter title or heading appears at the top of a page:

1. Click in the chapter title or heading.

2. Choose Format➪Paragraph.

3. Click the Text Flow tab.

4. Choose <u>P</u>age Break Before.

5. Click OK.

To make sure that text lines, paragraphs, or graphics stay on the same page:

1. Select the text lines. If you want to keep paragraphs together, either place the cursor in the paragraph that you want to tie to the following paragraph or select all the paragraphs except the last one.

2. Choose F<u>o</u>rmat⇨<u>P</u>aragraph.

3. Click the Text <u>F</u>low tab.

4. Click a Pagination check box:

- **Keep Lines Together:** Prevents the lines you selected from being broken across two pages.

- **Keep with Ne<u>x</u>t:** Ties the paragraph or paragraphs to the paragraph that follows so that they all stay on the same page.

5. Click OK.

Word 95 sometimes has to break a page early to make all your paragraphs and text stay together on the next page. That can create a lot of empty, forlorn white space.

What's more, forgetting where and when you choose Pagination options in a document is easy. If you notice pages breaking in weird places, click the Show/Hide ¶ button and look for small black squares in the margin. These squares represent pagination codes. You can always "deselect" Pagination options by opening the Paragraph dialog box and removing the check marks from the Pagination check boxes.

┌ Pagination codes

┌ **Breaking·the·Door·Down¶**

Gaining·a·toehold·in·the·Japanese·market·isn't·easy.·One·must· know·the·culture.·Japanese·business·practices·aren't·like·those·of· America,·where·aggression·and·daring·are·considered·virtues·and· are·rewarded·handsomely.·In·Japan,·cooperation·is·the·watchword· and·decisions·are·made·cautiously,·with·great·consideration·and· care.¶

¶

TIP

Whatever you do, don't remove the check mark from the Widow/Orphan Control check box in the Text Flow tab. This option keeps widows and orphans from appearing in documents. A *widow* is a very short line, usually one word, that appears at the end of a paragraph. The preceding figure contains a widow, the word *care*. Widows create a lot of ugly white space across the page.

An *orphan* is a single line of text at the start of a paragraph that appears at the very bottom of a page. Orphans sort of cheat the reader, because the reader can't tell how long the paragraph is until he or she turns the page.

"Landscape" Documents

A *landscape* document is one in which the page is wider than it is long, like a painting of a landscape. Most documents are printed in Portrait style, with the short sides of the page on the top and bottom. However, creating a landscape document is a good idea because a landscape document stands out from the usual crowd of portrait documents.

To turn the page on its ear and create a landscape document:

1. Choose File⇨Page Setup.

2. Click the Paper Size tab.

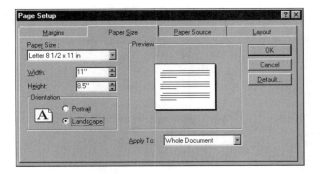

3. In the Orientation area, click the Landscape option button. The piece of paper in the Preview box turns on its side.

4. Make sure that Whole Document appears in the Apply To box, because it wouldn't do to create a document with both landscape and portrait pages.

5. Click OK.

See also "Printing on Different-Sized Paper" in Part IV to learn other ways of creating documents on different paper sizes and shapes.

Making Room to Bind a Document

If you intend to bind your document, you need to make room for the binding. Big plastic bindings eat into page margins and make the text beside the binding difficult to read. Lucky for you, Word 95 makes handling bindings easy:

1. Choose File⇨Page Setup.

2. On the Margins tab, click the up arrow beside the Gutter box. As you do so, watch the Preview box to see how the binding eats into your document. The longer the document, the more gutter space you need for binding.

3. If yours is a two-sided document with text printed on both sides of the paper, click the Mirror Margins check box and adjust the gutter accordingly.

4. Now that you can see how big the gutter is in the Preview box, adjust the Inside or Inside and Outside margin settings.

5. Click OK.

Click for binding

Watch this box!

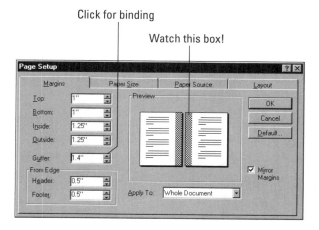

Part VII

Fancy and Esoteric Stuff

Everything in Part VII deserves a Cool Stuff icon. You'll
find instructions here for doing tasks that would take
hours and hours without Word 95's help. Most of the
tasks have to do with generating lists of one kind or
another — tables of contents, tables of figures, and
indexes. You'll also find some neat shortcuts for tracking
changes to documents and writing commentary on
documents.

In this part...

✔ **Commenting on a document with annotations and
  hidden text**

✔ **Generating tables of contents and other tables**

✔ **Creating an index**

✔ **Keeping track of revisions made to documents**

✔ **Creating and working with footnotes, endnotes, and
  cross-references**

Annotating a Document

An *annotation* is a note of explanation or commentary. In the old days, annotations were scribbled illegibly in the margins of books and documents, but, in Word 95, annotations are easy to read. What's more, each one is given the initials of the person who wrote it, so you always know whom an annotation came from. If you are putting together a proposal, you can pass it around the office and invite everyone to annotate it. If an annotator makes an especially good comment, you can include it in the main text merely by copying and pasting it.

To write an annotation:

1. Put the cursor in the word or sentence that you want to annotate.

2. Choose Insert⇨Annotation. A window opens at the bottom of the screen with annotations that have already been made and the initials of the annotators. The annotations are numbered.

Click to see comments by individual reviewers

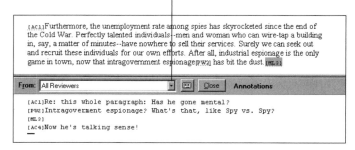

3. Type your annotation next to the square brackets with your initials in them. (If your initials don't appear in the brackets, choose Tools⇨Options, click the User Info tab, and type your initials in the Initials box.)

4. Click the Close button.

The fast way to see annotations is to click the Show/Hide ¶ button on the toolbar. When the square-bracketed, numbered, initialed annotations appear in the text, double-click the one you want to read. The Annotation window opens so you can read the annotation.

If an annotation is so good that it belongs in the document, simply select it in the Annotation window, drag it into the document, and reformat or rewrite it as necessary. To copy an annotation, hold down the Ctrl key as you drag it.

To delete an annotation, select it in the text and press the Delete key. The remaining annotations are renumbered. Unfortunately, you can't delete all the annotations in a document at once, so the best thing to do is to delete them one at a time as you finish reviewing them.

You can use the Edit⇨Go To command to find annotations in a document:

1. Choose Edit⇨Go To.

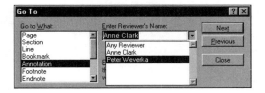

2. Click Annotation in the Go to What box.

3. Click the down arrow in the Enter Reviewer's Name box and choose a name if you want to see annotations made by a single reviewer.

4. Click the Next or Previous button to move through the document and find the annotation you want to review.

5. Click the Close button or press Esc when you're done.

Another way to annotate documents is to hide text. *See* "Hidden Text and Secret Messages" later in this part.

Creating a Table of Figures, Tables, or Equations

A table of figures, table of tables, or table of equations sometimes appears at the start of technical documents so that readers can refer to figures, tables, and equations quickly. As long as you use the Insert⇨Caption command to create captions for these things, you can generate tables automatically. (*See* "Putting Captions on Figures and Tables" later in this part if you'd like Word 95's help with captions.)

To generate a table of figures, tables, or equations:

1. Put the cursor where you want the table to go.

2. Choose Insert⇨Index and Tables.

Watch this box!

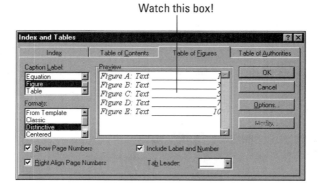

3. Click the Table of Figures tab.

4. Choose options on the tab. As you do so, watch the Preview box to see how your choices affect the table's appearance:

- **Caption Label:** Choose what kind of table you're creating.

- **Formats:** Choose a format from the list if you don't want to use the one from the template.

- **Show Page Numbers:** Includes the page numbers on the table.

- **Right Align Page Numbers:** Aligns the numbers along the right side of the table so that the ones and tens line up under each other.

- **Include Label and Number:** Includes the word *Figure*, *Table*, or *Equation* as well as the number or letter in the table caption.

- **Tab Leader:** Choose another leader, or no leader at all if you don't want a line of periods to appear between the caption and the number of the page on which it appears.

- **Options:** Lets you create tables from the styles used in your document or the fields found in the tables.

- **Modify:** You can modify the template's table of figures format by clicking the Modify button and creating a new TOF style of your own. When the Styles dialog box opens, choose the style you want to modify in the Styles box. Then click the Modify button and create a new Style in the Modify Style dialog box. *See* "Using styles for consistent formatting" in Part III to see how to create a new style.

5. Click OK when you're done.

If you add a figure, table, or equation to the document, or if you remove one, you can easily get an up-to-date table. Click in the table and press F9. A dialog box appears and asks how you want to update the table. If you've formatted the captions in any way, choose Update Page Numbers Only to keep your formats intact. Otherwise, click Update Entire table and click OK.

Generating a Table of Contents

A book-size document isn't worth very much without a table of contents. How else can readers find what they're looking for? Generating a table of contents with Word 95 is easy, as long as you give the headings in the document different styles — Heading 1, Heading 2, and so on.

Before you create your TOC, create a new section in which to put it and number the pages in the new section with Roman numerals. TOCs, including the TOC in this book, are usually numbered in this way. The first entry in the TOC should cite page number 1. If you don't take my advice and create a new section, the TOC will occupy the first few numbered pages of your document, and the number scheme will be thrown off.

To create a table of contents:

1. Place the cursor where you want the TOC to go.

2. Choose Insert⇨Index and Tables.

3. Click the Table of Contents tab in the Index and Tables dialog box.

Watch this box!

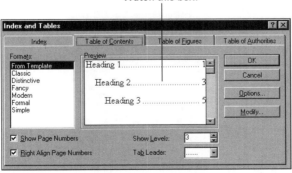

4. Choose options in the dialog box; watch the Preview box as you do so to see what effect your choices have.

5. Click OK when you're done.

The Table of Contents tab gives you lots of ways to control what goes in your TOC and what it looks like:

✦ **Show Page Numbers:** Uncheck this box if you want your TOC to be a simple list that doesn't refer to headings by page.

✦ **Right Align Page Numbers:** Aligns the page numbers along the right side of the TOC so that the ones and tens line up under each other.

✦ **Show Levels:** Determines how many heading levels are included in the TOC. Unless your document is a legal contract or other formal paper, enter a **2** or **3** here. A TOC is supposed to help readers find information quickly. Including lots of headings that take a long time to read through defeats the purpose of having a TOC.

✦ **Tab Leader:** A *leader* is the punctuation mark that appears between the heading and the page number the heading is on. If you don't want periods as the leader, choose another leader or choose (none).

✦ **Options:** Opens the Table of Contents Options dialog box so you can create TOC entries from the styles in your document. Click this button if you've created a Chapter Title style, for example. Scroll down the TOC Level box to find the style you want to include and type a level number in the box beside its name. Chapter titles should be given the 1 level. You can also include text in fields in the TOC by clicking the Table Entry Fields check box. Index entries and tables of figures, for example, can be included in the TOC with this check box. Click Reset if you get all tangled up and want to start over.

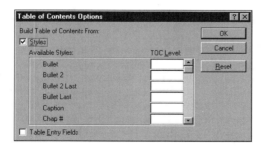

✦ **Modify:** Click this button if none of the TOC formats in the Formats box suits you and you want to try your hand at inventing a TOC style of your own. When you click Modify, the Style dialog box appears. In the Styles box, click the TOC level for which you want to create a style, and then click the Style dialog box's Modify button. You see the Modify Style dialog box. If you're adventurous enough to get this far, you probably already know how to create a new style. If you don't, *see* "Using styles for consistent formatting" in Part III.

Hidden Text and Secret Messages

Besides annotating, another way to make comments on a document is to make them with hidden text. (Annotations are explained at the start of this part.) Hidden text is not printed along with other text unless you tell Word 95 to print it. All you have to do to see hidden text is click the Show/Hide ¶ button.

To write hidden text and secret messages in a document:

1. Place the cursor where you want the text to go.

2. Choose Format⇨Font.

3. In the Effects area at the bottom of the Font dialog box, click the Hidden check box.

4. Click the OK button.

5. Type your secret message.

Dotted lines appear below hidden text on-screen. This advertising copywriter used hidden text to show the subliminal messages that the advertisement is meant to convey:

```
Summer's·coming·on·and·that·means·bathing·suit·time·
again·and·you·put·on·weight·since·last·summer,·no·doubt.·
Why·not·come·visit·us·at·the·Hayes·Street·Workout·
Center?·You'll·meet·lots·of·friendly·people·i.e.|·
attractive·members·of·the·opposite·sex.·Come·on.·You've·
got·nothing·to·lose·—·nothing·but·a·few·pounds,·that·is.¶
```

To see hidden text, either click the Show/Hide ¶ button or choose Tools⇨Options, click the View tab, and click Hidden Text in the Nonprinting Characters area of the Font dialog box. When it's time to hide the text again, either click the Show/Hide ¶ button or open the Options dialog box and remove the check mark from the Hidden Text check box.

If you'd like to print the hidden text in a document, make sure you won't embarrass yourself by printing it and then choose Tools⇨Options, click the Print tab, and click the Hidden Text check box in the Include with Document part of the dialog box.

Including a Database in a Document

Yes, you can import a database into a Word 95 document. If you
created the database with Microsoft Access, dBASE, or another
database application, you're in luck because Word 95 can usually
import comma-delimited and tab-delimited databases without any
difficulties. I say "usually" because you never quite know what a
database will do when you transplant it from one application to
another.

TIP Word 95 has tools for sorting, filtering, and choosing records in
databases. However, if you're importing the database from another
application, spare yourself a hassle and sort and filter the data there
before you bring it to Word 95.

When a database is imported into Word 95, it takes the form of a
table. To import a database:

1. Place the cursor where you want the database to go.

2. Choose Insert⇨Database. The Database dialog box appears:

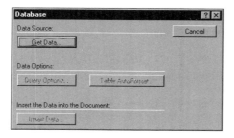

3. Click the Get Data button.

4. In the Open Data Source dialog box, find the data file you want to
import and click Open.

CROSS-REFERENCE *5.* Back at the Database dialog box, you can click the Query Options
button and fool with options for sorting, filtering, and selecting
records in the database, but if you took my advice and did those
tasks in the database application, you don't have to do that now.
***See** Word For Windows 95 For Dummies* (IDG Books Worldwide,
Inc.) if you need sorting and filtering advice.

6. Click the Table AutoFormat button.

7. In the Table AutoFormat dialog box, choose options for formatting the table and keep your eyes on the Preview box as you do
so. That box shows you what your database table will look like.

- **Formats to Apply:** These options apply formats to the table as a whole. Click the AutoFit check box if your database is a wide one and you want it to fit across the page.

- **Apply Special Formats To:** These options apply to parts of the table. *Heading row* is computerspeak for the top row of a table or database.

Watch this box!

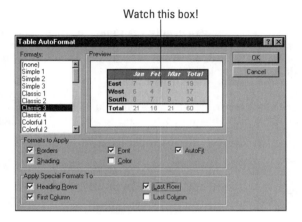

8. Click OK to close the Table AutoFormat dialog box.

9. Back at the Database dialog box, click the Insert Data button. The Insert Data dialog box appears:

10. Choose an Insert Records option. If you took my advice about tailoring the database before you imported it, click the All button. You can enter record numbers in the From and To boxes, but at this point that's kind of hard because you can't see the database and you probably don't know how the records are numbered.

11. Click the Insert Data as Field check box if you want to create a link between the database you're importing and your Word 95 document. If you choose this option, you can update your database table whenever the information in the original database changes.

12. Click OK. After a bit of hard-disk bumping and grinding, the database table appears in your document.

If you inserted your database as a field and need to update it, right-click the database and choose Update Field from the shortcut menu.

Indexing a Document

A good index is a thing of beauty. User manuals, reference works of any length, and reports that readers will refer to all require indexes. Except for the table of contents, the only way to find information in a long document is to look in the index.

An index entry can be formatted in many ways. You can cross-reference index entries, list a page range in an index entry, and break out an index entry into subentries and sub-subentries. To help you with your index, this figure explains indexing terminology:

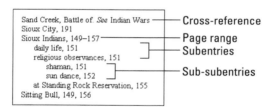

Marking index items in the document

There really is no fast way to mark items in a document for indexing, but the fastest way available is to create a *concordance file* and use it to tell Word 95 which topics and which words to include in the index. Using a concordance file, Word 95 runs through your document, finds all the topics in the concordance file and attaches index entries and page numbers to each topic.

The concordance file method does a quick-and-dirty job of creating an index. It can't handle cross-references between topics, however, without including a page number in the cross-reference. Nor can it list page ranges for index entries. Perhaps you want to be more thorough. In that case, you have to go through the document and mark index entries yourself. Both methods are described here.

If you opt for the concordance file method of creating an index, here's how to do it:

1. Click the New button or press Ctrl+N to open a new file.

2. Create a two-column table. To do that, either click the Insert Table button and choose two columns from the drop-down list, or choose Table⇨Insert Table and click OK.

3. In the first column, type a text item from your document that you want Word 95 to find for the index. What you enter here is not the index entry itself — just the topic of the entry. For example, to make an index entry on the Sioux Indians, type **Sioux** in the first column to have Word 95 find all occurrences of that word.

To be indexed, words in your document must be exact matches of the words in the first column. For example, if you enter **Ghost Dance Cult** in the first column but the name is *Ghost Dance cult* (with a lowercase *c*) in your document, the topic won't be indexed because Word 95 won't recognize it.

4. Press Tab to go to the second column of the table. This column is where you type the entry itself. For example, to create an index entry called "Sioux Indians," type **Sioux Indians**. You can create subentries by using a colon. For example, to make "Sioux Indians" a subentry of "Indians, North American," type **Indians, North American:Sioux**.

5. Go back to the first column and repeat steps 3 and 4 for your next index topic and entry. If you need more rows, right-click the table and choose Insert Rows from the shortcut menu. You can enter the topics and entries in any order. Word 95 alphabetizes them for you in the index.

6. When you're done creating the concordance file, save it. Your file should look something like this:

Custer	Custer, General George
Ghost Dance cult	Wovoka:Ghost Dance cult
Little Bighorn	Little Bighorn, Battle of
Sioux	Sioux Indians
Sitting Bull	Sitting Bull
Standing Rock	Sioux Indians:at Standing Rock Reservation
sun dance	Sioux Indians:sun dance
Wovoka	Wovoka

A fast way to create a concordance file is to open the file with the text you're indexing along with the concordance file, choose Window⇨Arrange All, and copy text from the document to the left-hand column of the concordance file.

After you create the concordance file, you can use it to mark the entries in the index:

1. Open the document with the text to be indexed.

2. Choose Insert⇨Index and Tables and click the Index tab, if necessary.

3. Click the AutoMark button.

4. In the Open Index AutoMark dialog box, find the concordance file and click Open.

A bunch of ugly field codes appear in your document. You can render them invisible by pressing the Show/Hide ¶ button. Now you can go ahead and generate the index.

Marking index items yourself is easier than it seems. Once you open the Mark Index Entry dialog box, it stays open so that you can scroll through your document and make entries. Using this method, you can enter cross-references and page ranges in index entries.

1. If you see a word in your document that you can use as a main, top-level entry, select it. You can save a little time that way, as you'll see shortly. Otherwise, if you don't see a word you can use, place the cursor in the paragraph whose topic you want to include in the index.

2. Press Alt+Shift+X. The Mark Index Entry dialog box appears. If you selected a word, it appears in the Main Entry box.

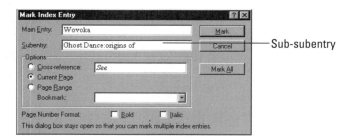
Sub-subentry

3. Choose how you want to handle this index entry. When you enter the text, don't put a comma or period after it. Word 95 does that when it generates the index. The text you enter will appear in your index.

- **Main Entry:** If you're entering a main, top-level entry, either leave the text in the Main Entry box (if it's already there), type new text to describe this entry, or edit the text that's already there. Leave the Subentry box blank.

- **Subentry:** To create a subentry, enter text in the Subentry box. The text will appear in the index below the Main Entry text, so make sure that there is text in the Main Entry box and that the subentry text fits under the main entry.

- **Sub-subentry:** A sub-subentry is the third level in the hierarchy. To create a sub-subentry, type the subentry, enter a colon, and type the sub-subentry.

4. Decide how to handle the page reference in the entry:

- **Cross-reference:** To go without a page reference and refer the reader to another index entry, click Cross-reference and type the other entry in the text box after the word *See*. What you type here appears in your index, so be sure that the topic you refer the reader to is really in the index.

- **Current Page:** Click this option to enter a single page number after the entry.

- **Page Range:** Click this option if you're indexing a subject that covers several pages in your document. A page range index entry looks something like this: "Sioux Indians, 45–49." To make a page range entry, you must create a bookmark for the range. Click outside the dialog box to get back to your document and select all the text in the page range. Then choose Edit⇨Bookmark, type a name in the Bookmark Name box (you may as well type the name of the index entry), and click Add. Back in the Mark Entry dialog box, click the Page Range option button, click the down arrow, and choose your bookmark from the list. Click Mark when you get to step 6, not Mark All.

5. You can boldface or italicize a page number or page range by clicking a Page Number Format check box. In some indexes, the page or page range where the topic is explained in the most depth is italicized or boldfaced so that readers can get to the juiciest parts first.

6. If you select a word in step 1, you can click Mark All to have Word 95 go through the document and mark all words identical to the one in the Main Entry box. Click Mark to put this single entry in the index.

7. Click outside the Mark Index Entry dialog box and find the next topic or word you want to mark for the index.

8. Repeat steps 3 through 7 until you've marked all your index entries, and then click Cancel to close the Mark Index Entry dialog box.

Generating an index

After you mark the index entries, it's time to generate the index:

1. Place the cursor where you want the index to go, most likely at the end of the document. You might type the word **Index** and format the word in a decorative way.

2. Choose Insert⇨Index and Tables and click the Index tab, if necessary.

Watch this box!

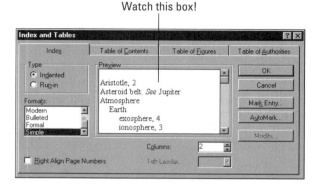

3. Choose options in the Index and Tables dialog box. As you do so, watch the Preview box to see what happens.

4. When you're done, click OK.

Here are the options in the Index and Tables dialog box:

✦ **Type:** Choose Run-in if you want subentries and sub-subentries to appear flush with the left margin like main entries. Otherwise, stick with the Indented option to indent them.

✦ **Formats:** Word 95 offers a number of attractive index layouts. You can choose one from the list.

✦ **Right Align Page Numbers:** Normally, page numbers appear immediately after entries and are separated from entries by a comma, but you can right-align the entries so they line up under one another with this option.

✦ **Columns:** Stick with 2, unless you don't have subentries or sub-subentries and you can squeeze three columns on the page.

✦ **Tab Leader:** Some index formats (such as Formal) place a *leader* between the entry and the page number. A leader is a series of dots or dashes. If you're working with a format that has a leader, you can choose a leader from the drop-down list.

✦ **Modify:** Click this button if you're adventurous and want to create an index style of your own. You must choose From Template in the Formats box in order to do so. In the Style dialog box, choose an Index level style and then click the Style dialog box's Modify button to get to the Modify Style dialog box and create a style of your own. *See* "Using styles for consistent formatting" in Part III if you need help creating styles.

Editing an index

Inevitably, something doesn't come out right after you generate an index. You can go in and fix it by hand, but that won't solve your problem in the long run if you intend to work on your document some more and you have to generate the index again.

¶ Index field markers are enclosed in angle brackets with the letters *XE* and the text of the index entry in quotation marks, like so: `{ XE: "Sioux Indians:sun dance" }`. To edit an index marker, click the Show/Hide ¶ button to see the field markers and find the one you need to edit. Here's a quick way to find index field markers:

1. Choose Edit⇨Go To.

2. Click Field in the Go to What box.

3. Type **XE** in the Enter Field Name box.

4. Click the Next button until you find the marker you want to edit.

If you're nervous about editing fields (I am), you can erase the one that's troubling your index and mark it all over again. To delete a field marker, select it and press Delete.

To update an index after you edit it, either right-click the index and choose Update Field from the shortcut menu or click the index and press F9.

Keeping Track of Document Revisions

When a lot of hands go into revising a document, figuring out who made revisions to what is impossible. More important, it's impossible to tell what the original draft looked like.

To help you keep track of document revisions, Word 95 offers the Tools⇨Revisions command. When revision marks are turned on, all changes to the document are recorded in different colors, with one color for each reviser. You can see precisely where revisions were made and who made them. Then you can accept or reject each revision. You can also compare the first draft of a document with subsequent drafts to see where revisions were made.

To show where revisions were made, a vertical line appears in the margin of the document. Meanwhile, new text is underlined, and a line is drawn through text that has been deleted. To give you an idea of what revision marks look like, here are the first two lines of Vladimir Nabokov's autobiography *Speak, Memory* with revision marks to show where he made changes to his first draft.

> The cradle rocks above an abyss, and ~~Vulgar~~ common sense
> ~~assures~~ tell<u>s</u> us that our existence is but a brief ~~strip~~
> <u>crack</u> of light between two eternities of ~~complete~~ darkness.
> Although the two are identical twins, <u>man, as a rule,</u> ~~maybe~~
> ~~we~~ views the prenatal ~~one~~ <u>abyss</u> with ~~considerably~~ more <u>calm</u>
> ~~equanimity~~ than the one <u>he is</u> ~~we are~~ heading for (at some
> forty-five hundred heartbeats an hour).

Marking your revisions

To use revision marks in a document:

1. Either double-click MRK on the status bar or choose
Tools⇨Revisions. The Revisions dialog box appears.

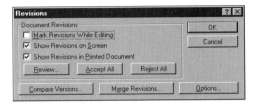

2. Click the Mark Revisions While Editing check box.

3. If you don't want to see the revision marks on-screen, click the
Show Revisions on Screen check box to remove the check mark.
Revisions to the document are recorded with this option, but
they aren't shown. In a document with a lot of revisions, choose
this option to work without all that clutter on-screen.

4. Click OK.

Now you can start revising. If you are the first author to have a crack
at this document, your revisions appear in blue. If you are the second,
they appear in green. Word 95 can tell when a new reviser has gotten
hold of a document, and it assigns a new color accordingly.

To choose a revision color of your own:

1. Double-click MRK on the status bar.

2. Click the Options button in the Revisions dialog box.

3. In the Revisions tab of the Options dialog box, go to the Inserted
Text area, click the down arrow on the Color drop-down list, and
choose a new color.

4. Click OK.

You can also change how revisions are marked by choosing options in the Deleted Text and Revised Lines areas of the dialog box.

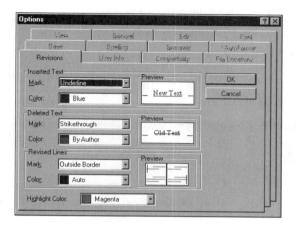

When a reviser chooses a new color for revision marks, the color scheme breaks down, and Word 95 stops assigning new colors to new revisers. You can end up with a document in which revisions from many different authors appear in the same color or in only one or two colors. To reassign a different color to each author who has worked on a document, open the Options dialog box and choose By Author in the Color drop-down lists in both the Inserted Text and Deleted Text areas.

Comparing and merging documents

The fastest way to handle revision marks may be to compare or merge the revised document with its forebear. To do so, double-click MRK on the status bar and click either the Compare Versions or the Merge Versions button in the Revisions dialog box:

✦ **Compare Versions:** Choose this option if the original document is saved under a different name or is saved in a different directory. In the Compare Versions dialog box, find the original file, select it, and choose Open. Revision marks appear on the changes you've made to the document.

✦ **Merge Versions:** Choose this option if you have the original document and want to see what others have done to it. In the Merge Revisions dialog box, click the revised version of the file and click Open. Marked revisions appear in your original copy of the document.

Accepting and rejecting revisions

Now that the revisions have been made, you can decide what to do about them. To review the revisions one at a time:

1. Double-click MRK on the status bar or choose Tools⇨Revisions.

2. Click Review in the Revisions dialog box. The Review Revisions dialog box appears:

Who made the revision

3. Click a Find button to start searching for revisions marks. Word highlights a revision on-screen. The name of the person who made the revision appears in the Description box.

4. Click Accept to keep it or Reject to reverse it.

5. Click a Find button to find the next revision and either reject or accept it. You can click the Find Next After Accept/Reject check box to speed up this business. With this choice, you don't have to keep clicking Find buttons, because Word 95 goes straight to the next revision after you click the Accept or Reject button.

6. Keep accepting or rejecting. If you change your mind about a revision, click the Undo Last button.

7. Click Close or press Esc when you're done.

If you trust your colleagues and have total faith in their revisions, you can accept their revisions in one fell swoop. Click the Accept All button on the Revisions dialog box. When Word asks whether you really want to accept them all, click Yes.

You can reject all the revisions just as easily. Click Reject All in the Revisions dialog box.

Putting Captions on Figures and Tables

Word 95 has a special feature for putting captions on tables, figures, equations, graphs, and a number of other things. Of course, you can add captions yourself, but by letting Word 95 do it, you can compile the captions in tables. At the beginning of a user manual, for example, you can have a table called "Figures in This Manual." Readers can refer to the table when they want to find a figure.

To put a caption on a figure, table, equation, graph, or anything else, for that matter:

1. Either place the cursor where you want the caption to go or select the item for which you want to write a caption.

2. Choose Insert⇨Caption. The Caption dialog box appears.

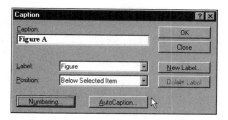

3. In the Label drop-down list, choose which kind of item you're creating a caption for. To create a caption for something that is not on the list, click the New Label button, type a label in the Label box, and click OK.

4. If you selected the item before you chose Insert⇨Caption, choose Below Selected Item or Above Selected Item in the Position drop-down menu.

5. Click the Numbering button if you want a different numbering scheme than the one shown in the Caption box. In the Caption Numbering dialog box, choose a number scheme from the Format menu and look at the examples at the bottom to see what your choices mean. Click the Include Chapter Number check box and choose a style and separator if you want to include chapter numbers in the numbering scheme. Click OK to get back to the Caption dialog box.

6. Click the AutoCaption button if you want Word 95 to put captions on new tables or equations as you create them. The AutoCaption dialog box appears if you make this choice. Click an item in the Add Caption When Inserting box and click OK.

7. Click OK to insert your caption.

See "Creating a Table of Figures, Tables, or Equations" earlier in this part to see how to compile the captions in tables.

Putting Cross-References in a Document

Cross-references are very handy indeed. They tell readers where to go to find more information on a topic. The problem with cross-references, however, is that the thing being cross-referenced really has to be there. If you refer readers to a heading called "The Cat's Pajamas" on page 93 and neither the heading nor the page exists, readers curse and tell you where to go, instead of the other way around.

Fortunately for you, Word 95 lets you know when you make errant cross-references. You can refer readers to headings, page numbers, footnotes, endnotes, captions, and plain old paragraphs. If you delete the text that a cross-reference refers to and render the cross-reference invalid, Word 95 tells you about it the next time you update your cross-references. Best of all, if the page number that a cross-reference refers to changes, so does the cross-reference.

You can refer to text in documents other than the one you're working on, as long as both documents are part of the same master document (*see* "Master Document for Really Big Jobs" in Part V to find out about master documents).

To create a cross-reference:

1. Write the first part of the cross-reference text. For example, you could write **To learn more about these cowboys of the pampas, see page** and then enter a blank space. The blank space separates the word *page* from the page number you're about to enter with the Insert➪Cross-reference command. If you are referring to a heading, write something like **For more information, see ".** Don't enter a blank space this time, because the heading text will appear right after the double-quotation mark.

2. Choose Insert➪Cross-reference. The Cross-reference dialog box appears:

3. Choose what type of item you're referring to in the Reference Type menu. If you're referring to a plain old paragraph, choose Bookmark. Then click outside the dialog box, scroll to the paragraph you're referring to, and place a bookmark there (with the Edit⇨Bookmark command).

4. Your choice in the Insert Reference To box determines whether the reference is to text, a page number, or a numbered item. The options in this box are different, depending on what you chose in step 3.

- **Text:** Choose this option (Heading Text, Bookmark Text, and so on) to include text in the cross-reference. For example, choose Heading Text if your cross-reference is to a heading.

- **Page Number:** Choose this option to insert a page number in the cross-reference.

- **Number:** Choose this option to insert a numbered item, such as a footnote or figure number.

5. In the For Which box, tell Word 95 where the thing you're referring to is located. To do so, select a heading, bookmark, footnote, endnote, equation, figure, graph, or table in the menu. You may have to use the scroll bar to find the one you want.

6. Click Insert.

7. Click the Close button or press Esc.

8. Back in your document, enter the rest of the cross-reference text.

If you see an ugly code in your document instead of the reference text or page number, right-click the cross-reference field and choose Toggle Field Codes from the shortcut menu.

When you finish creating your document, update all the cross-references. To do that, press Ctrl and click in the left margin to select the entire document. Then right-click in the document and choose Update Field from the shortcut menu.

If the thing referred to in a cross-reference is no longer in your document, you see `Error! Reference source not found` where the cross-reference should be. Investigate this urgent matter and either delete the cross-reference or make a new one.

Putting Footnotes and Endnotes in Documents

A *footnote* is a reference, bit of explanation, or comment that appears at the bottom of the page and is referred to by a number or symbol in the text. An *endnote* is the same thing, only it appears at the end of the chapter or document. If you've written a scholarly paper of any kind, you know what a drag footnotes and endnotes are.

Word 95 takes some of the drudgery out of footnotes and endnotes. If you delete or add one, for example, all the others are renumbered. And you don't have to worry about long footnotes, because Word 95 adjusts the page layout to make room for them. You can change the numbering scheme of footnotes and endnotes at will.

Inserting a footnote or endnote

To insert a footnote or endnote in a document:

1. Place the cursor in the text where you want the note's symbol or number to appear.

2. Choose Insert⇨Footnote. The Footnote and Endnote dialog box appears.

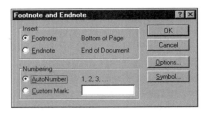

3. Choose whether you're entering a footnote or an endnote in the Insert area of the dialog box.

4. In the Numbering area, click AutoNumber if you want Word 95 to number the notes automatically or Custom Mark to insert a symbol of your own. If you want to insert a symbol, click the Symbol button and choose one from the Symbol dialog box. If you go this route, you have to enter a symbol each time you insert a note. Not only that, but you may have to enter two or three symbols for the second and third notes on each page or document.

5. Click OK. A notes box opens at the bottom of the screen with the cursor beside the number of the note you're about to enter (if you don't see this box, switch to Normal view by clicking the Normal view button in the lower-left corner of the screen or choosing View⇨Normal).

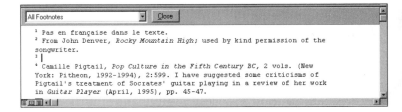

6. Type your footnote or endnote.

7. Click Close or press Esc when you're done.

If you don't like how Word 95 formats footnotes or endnotes, create a Footnote Text or Endnote Text style of your own. For example, note numbers are superscripted. You may want to make them plain numbers followed by periods.

Changing the numbering scheme and position of notes

Changing the numbering scheme and positioning of endnotes and footnotes is quite easy:

1. Choose Insert⇨Footnote.

2. Click the Options button in the Footnote and Endnote dialog box. The Note Options dialog box appears.

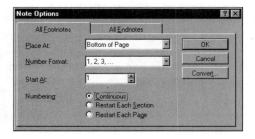

3. Click the All Footnotes or All Endnotes tab. The options on these tabs are nearly the same:

- **Place At:** For footnotes, choose Bottom of Page to put footnotes at the bottom of the page no matter where the text ends; choose Beneath Text to put footnotes directly below the last text line on the page. For endnotes, choose End of Section if your document is divided into sections (such as chapters) and you want endnotes to appear at the backs of sections; choose End of Document to put endnotes at the very back of the document.

- **Number Format:** Choose A B C, i ii iii, or another numbering scheme. You can also enter symbols by choosing the last option on this drop-down menu.

- **Start At:** To start numbering the notes at a place other than 1, A, or i, enter **2**, **B**, **ii**, or whatever in this box.

- **Numbering:** To number the notes continuously from the start of your document to the end, choose Continuous. Choose Restart Each Section to begin anew at each section of your document. For footnotes, you can begin anew on each page by choosing Restart Each Page.

- **Convert:** This very convenient button is for fickle scholars who suddenly decide that their endnotes should be footnotes or vice versa. Click it and choose an option in the Convert Notes dialog box to turn footnotes into endnotes, turn endnotes into footnotes, or — in documents with both endnotes and footnotes — make the endnotes footnotes and the footnotes endnotes.

4. Click OK in the Note Options dialog box.

5. Click OK in the Footnote and Endnote dialog box.

Deleting, moving, and editing notes

If a devious editor tells you that a footnote or endnote is in the wrong place, that you don't need a note, or that you need to change the text in a note, all is not lost.

✦ **Editing:** To edit a note, select and double-click its number or symbol in the text. The notes box appears at the bottom of the screen. Edit the note at this point.

✦ **Moving:** To move a note, select its number or symbol in the text and either drag it to a new location or cut and paste it to a new location.

✦ **Deleting:** To delete a note, select its number or symbol and press the Delete key.

Footnotes and endnotes are renumbered when you move or delete them.

Part VIII

Potpourri

On the TV show *Jeopardy,* the last column on the question board is sometimes called "Potpourri." That's where they put oddball questions that can't fit in any category. Part VIII is called "Potpourri," too, because the topics covered here don't fit in the other seven parts of the book.

Some of the tasks in this part are absolutely essential; others are downright wacky. But maybe I'm being judgmental, as we say in California, and all this stuff is actually very useful. I should let you decide what is and what isn't useful in Part VIII.

In this part...

✔ Backing up files so you have copies in case of an emergency

✔ Finding a lost file

✔ Getting information about a document

✔ Highlighting important text in a document

✔ Importing files from and exporting files to other word processors

✔ Including video and sound in documents

✔ Protecting your files with passwords

Backing Up Your Work

If an elephant steps on your computer or your computer breaks down and can't be repaired, you lose all the files you worked so hard to create. You have to start from scratch and create your files all over again, unless you backed them up. *Backing up* means to make a copy of a file and put it on a floppy disk, tape drive, or other place from which you can retrieve files in the event of a fire, locust attack, pestilence, coffee spill, computer breakdown, or other emergency.

Besides backing up files to a floppy disk or tape drive, you can back up files in special directories on your hard disk. The disadvantage of backing up this way, however, is that the files are still on your computer. If your computer breaks down altogether, you can't get your files back. However, you can recover them if there is a power failure or other untoward event that doesn't damage your computer.

Backing up to a floppy disk or tape drive

To back up a file to a location outside your computer, you leave Word 95 and do the job with Windows 95:

1. Close the file if it is open.

2. Open the Explorer utility in Windows 95. To do this, click the Start button, choose Programs, and choose Windows Explorer at the bottom of the Programs list. The Windows Explorer window appears on-screen.

3. Find the file you want to back up. To get to my Windows 95 files, I click the plus sign next to MS Office in the All Folders pane on the left side of the Explorer window. Then I click the plus sign next to Winword to see my Winword folders. Then I click the folder with the file I want to back up. When I click the folder, the files in the folder appear in the Contents Of window pane on the right side of the screen.

4. When you see the file you're backing up, click and drag it to the place where you will store the backup copy. To store it on a floppy disk, for example, drag it to the Floppy icon at the top of the All Folders window pane and release the mouse button.

The Copying message box appears. It tells you that the file is being copied and shows a picture of pieces of paper being flung from one folder to another.

Now you can get the file back by copying it from the floppy disk or tape drive to your new computer. Be sure to save your floppy disk or backup tape in a safe place away from your computer. A fire, for example, would destroy your computer and your backup files if you keep your backups on the desk next to your computer.

If you don't know how to handle files in Windows 95, by all means get a copy of Andy Rathbone's *Windows 95 For Dummies* (IDG Books Worldwide, Inc.).

Backing up files in Word 95

You can recover files that have been backed up or saved automatically if you accidentally unplug the computer or a power failure occurs. To tell Word 95 to back up and save files automatically:

1. Choose Tools⇨Options.

2. Click the Save tab of the Options dialog box.

3. Click the Always Create Backup Copy check box.

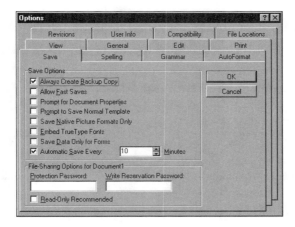

4. Click the Automatic Save Every check box and enter a number in the Minutes box to tell Word 95 how often to save the documents you work on.

5. Click OK.

Restoring a backup copy of a file

After you choose the Always Create Backup Copy and Automatic Save Every options, you can get copies of files after a power failure. So why would you choose one option over the other, or both options? Here's why:

✦ **Automatic Save Every:** With this option, Word 95 makes a second copy of your file every few minutes (depending on what you enter in the Minutes box). If a power failure occurs, you can restore the copy of your file that was saved a few minutes ago. On the other hand, the backup copy of the file is erased when you close the original file. You can't resort to the backup copy if the original file gets mangled or is rendered inoperable.

✦ **Always Create Backup Copy:** With this option, Word makes a second copy of your file and keeps it in the same folder as the original. However, the backup copy is made only when you, and not Word 95, save the file. If a power failure occurs, you can't recover the work you did in the last few minutes, although you can recover the version of the file that was saved the last time *you* saved the file. What's more, backup copies made with this option eat up a lot of disk space.

Recovering a file that was saved automatically

Suppose a power failure occurs. To recover a file that Word 95 saved automatically:

1. Start Word 95. All the documents that you were working on when lightning struck are opened on-screen.

2. Choose File➪Save As.

3. Click the Save button in the Save As dialog box.

4. Click Yes when Word 95 asks whether you want to replace the existing document.

The work you did in the last few minutes is lost, but the work that was complete the last time Word 95 saved the file automatically is restored.

If that technique for restoring an automatically saved file doesn't work, try this one:

1. Start Word 95.

2. Click the Open button, press Ctrl+N, or choose File⇨Open to display the Open dialog box.

3. Find the Temp folder in the Windows folder and click on it.

4. Click the down arrow on the Files of type box at the bottom of the screen and choose All Files.

5. Documents that were recovered when the power failed have the *.asd* extension. Open the document you want to recover, if it's there.

6. Follow steps 2 through 4 in the preceding instruction list.

Opening a backup copy of a file

To open the backup copy of a file after a power failure or other electrical accident:

1. Click the Open button, press Ctrl+N, or choose File⇨Open to display the Open dialog box.

2. Go to the folder where the original file was stored.

3. Click the down arrow on the Files of type box at the bottom of the screen and choose All Files.

4. Look for the backup copy and click it. Backup copy names start with the words *Backup of* and end with the *.wbk* extension.

5. Click Open.

Finding a Missing File

Occasionally, you forget the name of a file you want to open. Or you remember the name but forget the name of the folder you put the file in. When that happens, you can search for the file with menus in the Open dialog box:

1. Click the Open button, press Ctrl+N, or choose File⇨Open to get the Open dialog box.

2. Choose options at the bottom of the dialog box:

- **File name:** Enter the filename if you know it. If you vaguely remember the name, you can use wildcards to help with the search (*see* "Searching with Wildcards" in Part V to learn how to use wildcards). If you're utterly confused, don't worry. You can leave this box blank.

- **Files of type:** Click the down arrow and choose the type of file you're looking for. Most likely, it is Word Documents, but you can choose All Files or another option.

- **Text or property:** If you can remember a word or phrase from the document you're looking for, enter it here in quotation marks. For example, type **Dear Mom** if you're searching for a letter to your mother.

- **Last modified:** Click the down arrow and choose an option that best describes when you last saved the file.

3. Click the Find Now button. The file or files that match the criteria you just entered appear in the Open dialog box.

4. Click a file and choose Open to open it.

If Word 95 can't find a file that matches your criteria, 0 files(s) found appears in the lower-left corner of the Open dialog box. Change the criteria by clicking the New Search button and starting all over again.

 Windows 95 has a sleek, sophisticated way to look for lost files (the Find command on the Start menu). Get a copy of *Windows 95 For Dummies* (IDG Books Worldwide, Inc.) if you want to learn how to find files with Windows 95.

Getting Information about a Document

 Word 95 keeps information about your documents. You can find out how long you've worked on a document, how many times you've saved it, when you created it, and how many words it contains, among other things. You can also enter words to help Word 95 find your document if it is lost and change the author name and initials that the Tools⇨Revisions command uses to keep track of who makes revisions to documents.

To get the stats on a document:

1. Choose File⇨Properties.

2. Click the tabs to review or make changes on them.

3. Click OK.

The Statistics tab tells when the document was created, when and who last saved it, and how much work has gone into it in terms of time, pages, words, and characters, among other things.

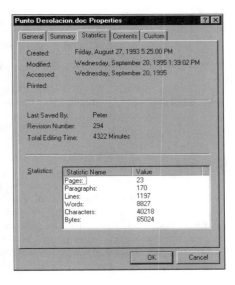

The Summary tab lists the author, title, and other pertinent informa- tion. If you think that you might lose your file someday, enter words in the Category and Keywords boxes to help Windows 95 find the file. Click the Save Preview Picture box to put a picture of the first page of the document in the Open dialog box instead of the standard Word 95 document icon.

The General tab tells you how long the file is and whether it's an archive, read-only, hidden, or system file.

The Contents tab tells you which subdocuments are in the file, if your file is a master document.

The Custom tab lets you create other means of keeping statistics on your documents.

Highlighting Parts of a Document

One way to call attention to the most important parts of a document is to highlight them. You can do that very easily with the Highlight button on the Formatting toolbar:

1. Scroll to the part of the document you want to highlight.

2. Click the Highlight button. The cursor changes into a fat pencil.

3. Drag the cursor over the text you want to highlight.

4. Click the Highlight button again when you're done.

Highlight marks are printed along with the text. To get rid of them:

1. Select the document or the text from which you want to remove the highlights.

2. Click the down arrow to open the Highlight color menu.

3. Click None.

Importing and Exporting Files

Word 95 makes it easy to use files from other Microsoft Office applications, from other versions of Microsoft Word (including Macintosh versions), from Write and Works, and from WordPerfect 5 and 6. Other files are a different story. For example, Word 95 is not on speaking terms with Ami Pro, not to mention antique word processors like WordStar and XYWrite.

Exporting files to the same programs from which it's easy to import files is simple. Your friends who have WordPerfect 5 and 6, for example, can use your files, but colleagues who have other word processors may well have to use stripped-down versions of your files that contain the text but none of the formats.

Even when you import or export a file successfully, some things get lost. For example, special characters and symbols often don't translate well. Nor do certain fonts. Carefully proofread files that you've imported or exported to make sure that everything came out right.

Importing a file

To import a file, you open it and let Word 95 turn it into a Word 95 file:

1. Click the Open button, press Ctrl+N, or choose File⇨Open to display the Open dialog box.

2. Find the file you want to import in the Open dialog box and click it.

3. Click the down arrow in the Files of type box and see whether the kind of file you want to import is on the list. If it is, click it. If it isn't, you can always click the Text Files option. With this option, all formats such as boldfacing and fonts are stripped from the file, but at least you get to keep the text.

4. Click Open.

Here's one way to get around file-importing impasses: If the application you want to import the file from works in Windows 95, open the application, open the file you want to copy, and copy the parts of the file you need to the Clipboard. Then copy what is on the Clipboard into Word 95.

Another way to get around the problem of not being able to import a file is to see whether the other application can save files in Microsoft Word format. If it can, save the file as a Microsoft Word file in the other application and then open it in Word 95.

Exporting a file

To export a file so that someone with another kind of word processor can use it, you save the file in a new format:

1. Choose File⇨Save As.

2. Find the file you want to export in the Save As dialog box and click it.

3. Click the down arrow in the Save as type menu and see whether the kind of file you want to export is on the list. If it is on the list, choose it. If it isn't, choose either Rich Text Format or Text Only with Line Breaks:

• Rich Text Format retains the formatting of the text, but some word processors can't understand it.

• In case worse comes to worst, Text Only with Line Breaks strips out all the formatting but retains the text and line breaks.

4. Click Save.

Including Video Clips and Sound in Documents

Video and sound are way, way too complex for this book. But if you want to bravely go where few nerds have gone before and include sound or video in a document, here are the basic steps:

1. Place the cursor where you want the sound or animation to go.

2. Choose Insert⇨Object. The Object dialog box appears.

Read the description

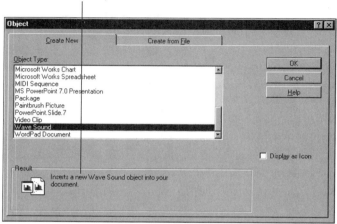

3. In the Object Type box, choose what you want to insert. The Result box at the bottom of the dialog box describes the different objects you can insert.

4. Click OK.

Depending on what you choose in step 3, Word 95 opens either another application or a special window for creating the sound byte or video sequence. You're on your own, and may the force be with you.

Protecting Your Work with Passwords

To keep jealous coworkers, your spouse, your boss, and unauthorized biographers from opening a file, you can protect it with a password. You can also allow others to view a document but not make changes to it unless they have the password. You can even protect parts of a document with the Tools⇨Protect Document command.

Keeping others from opening a file

To keep others from opening a document unless they have the password:

1. Open the document.

2. Choose Tools⇨Options and click the Save tab in the Options dialog box.

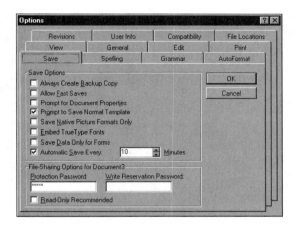

3. Type your password in the Protection Password box. Instead of letters, asterisks appear in the box in case a ne'er-do-well, leprechaun, or imp is looking over your shoulder. Passwords can be 15 characters long. If you include upper- and lowercase letters in your password, remember them well, because you have to reproduce your password exactly whenever you open this file.

4. Click OK.

5. In the Confirm Password dialog box, type the password again. If you don't enter it correctly, Word 95 tells you so and sends you back to the Options dialog box.

6. Click OK in the Confirm Password dialog box.

It almost goes without saying, but you must never, never forget your password. If you forget it, you simply cannot open the file again!

Everybody has different advice for choosing a password that isn't likely to be forgotten or discovered, and everybody agrees that you shouldn't use your name or the names of family members or pets, because miscreants try those names first when they try to crack open a file. Here's a good tip for choosing passwords: Pick your favorite foreign city and spell it backwards. My favorite foreign city is in France. If I needed a password, it would be **siraP**.

Opening a password-protected file

To open a file that has been given a password:

1. Open the file as you normally would. The Password dialog box appears.

2. Type the password and click OK.

If Word 95 tells you that it can't open the file because you've given the wrong password, you may have entered it with the wrong combination of upper- and lowercase characters. Try again using different capital letters and lowercase letters.

Removing a password

To remove a password, all you have to do is this:

1. Open the file.

2. Choose Tools⇨Options.

3. Click the Save tab.

4. Delete the asterisks from the Protection Password box.

5. Click OK.

Keeping others from changing a file

Besides keeping others from looking at a file, you can keep them from making changes to a file unless they have the password. This way, others can open the file, but they must have the password in order to edit it.

1. Open the document.

2. Choose Tools⇨Options and click the Save tab in the Options dialog box.

3. Type your password in the Write Reservation Password dialog box. The usual asterisks appear as you type the password.

4. Click OK.

5. In the Confirm Password dialog box, type the password again.

6. Click OK.

When someone other than yourself tries open this file, he or she sees this dialog box:

By entering the correct password and clicking OK, the other user can view and make changes to the file. If the other user doesn't have the password, he or she can still view the file by clicking the Read Only button.

Protecting parts of a document from changes

With Word 95's Tools⇨Protect Document command, you can prevent others from making changes in various ways. You can keep users who don't have the password from changing annotations and forms, and you can also force all changes made to the document to be recorded with revision marks. Here's how:

1. Open the document you want to protect.

2. Choose Tools⇨Protect Document. The Protect Document dialog box appears:

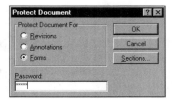

3. In the Protect Document For area, choose how you want to protect the file:

- **Revisions:** All changes made to the document are recorded with revision marks. This way, you always know where changes were made.

- **Annotations:** Reviewers can make their own annotations but can't change the annotations that are there already.

- **Forms:** Users can fill in form fields, but they can't change the text of the form.

4. If you want to protect the forms in only one or two sections in a document, make sure that the Forms options button is selected, click the Sections button, and click to remove the check marks from the sections you *don't* want to protect. Then click OK.

5. Enter a password in the Password box. Passwords can be 15 characters long. Remember this password and the exact combination of upper- and lowercase letters, because you and other users need to type it the same way when you want to make changes to annotations or forms or make changes without the revision marks showing.

6. Click OK to close the Protect Document dialog box.

Now users have to enter the correct password to change existing annotations or forms or make changes without revision marks.

To "unprotect" a document so that users can make changes at will, choose Tools⇨Unprotect Document.

Tips for Learning Word

You must have noticed the Tip of the Day that appears along the top of documents when you first start Word 95:

To keep it from cluttering your screen after you read it, click the TipWizard button in the upper, upper right corner of the screen between the Zoom Control box and the Help button.

That other light bulb, the one to the right of the Tip of the Day with a question mark next to it, is called the Show Me button. Click it if you're from Missouri or if the tip arouses your interest and you want to know more about what the Tip of the Day says.

You can keep Tips of the Day from appearing when you start Word 95 by following these steps:

1. Choose Tools⇨Options.

2. Click the General tab.

3. Remove the check mark from the TipWizard Active check box.

Techie Talk

AutoCorrect: Word 95 "autocorrects" what it thinks are errors in documents. Certain words are AutoCorrected, as are capitalization errors.

cell: The box that is formed in a table where a row and column intersect. Each cell holds one data item.

check box: A square box inside a dialog box. Click an option's check box to place a check mark in the box and activate the option. Click again to remove the check mark and render the option dormant.

click: To press the left mouse button once. Not to be confused with *clique,* a like-minded collection of high school students who dress and talk the same way. *See also* right-click.

clip art: Graphics and pictures that can be imported into a computer file.

Clipboard: A holding tank to which you can copy or move text and graphics. Text and graphics can be pasted from the Clipboard into a document.

crop: To cut off part of a graphic.

curb feeler: A flexible metal rod that was attached to the right rear bumper of many pre-1955 cars. Curb feelers helped with parallel parking, as drivers heard a scraping noise when their cars came too close to the curb.

cursor: An on-screen symbol that tells you what the computer is doing. Cursors include the insertion point, the vertical line that blinks on and off and tells you where text goes when you press the keys, and the mouse cursor, which looks like an arrow when you move the mouse over something you can choose, or like a large egotistical *I* when it is in a document window. Also, someone who curses at a computer screen.

dialog box: A box that appears on-screen when Word 95 needs more information to complete a task. Fill in the dialog box and click the OK button to give a command. *See also* check box, drop-down list, option button, radio button.

document: A letter, report, announcement, or proclamation that you create with Word. Any file you create with Word 95 is considered a document.

double-click: To click twice with the left mouse button.

drag and drop: The fastest way to copy or move text from one place to another. Select the text, drag it to a new location, and drop it there.

drop-down list: A menu box with a down arrow at its side. Click the down arrow, and a menu appears with options you can choose.

field: A code in a file that represents information that varies. For example, if you put a "today's date" field at the top of a letter you write on July 31, 1996, but print the letter on August 5, 1996, the letter is dated August 5, 1996. Also, a flat place where soccer is played or crops are grown.

file extension: The three-character extension following the period in filenames. Word 95 files have the *.doc* (document) extension. Each type of computer file has its own three-letter file extension.

font: A typeface design of a particular size and format.

footer: A line at the bottom of each page of a document that includes the document's name, the page number, or similar information. *See also* header.

function keys: The 10 or 12 keys along the top of the keyboard. You use the function keys to give commands.

gutter: In a bound document, the part of the paper that the binding eats into. Also, in a newspaper-style document, the space between columns.

header: A line at the top of the pages of a document that lists the document's name, the page number, or similar information. *See also* footer.

header row: The labels along the top row of a table or database that explain what is in the columns below.

hot key: The underlined letter in a command name. Press the hot key or Alt+hot key to execute a command quickly.

kerning: To move a pair of letters farther apart or closer together.

leading: The vertical distance between two lines of type.

margin: The empty space on a page between the text and the top, bottom, left, and right borders of the page.

mouse: The soap-shaped thing on your desk that you roll to make the mouse cursor move on-screen. If you reach for your mouse and feel fur or hear a squeaking sound, you should stop eating at your desk. The mouse has a left and right button. *See also* click, cursor, right-click.

object: A catchall term for something that can be put in a Word 95 document that isn't related to text — for example, sound bytes and graphics.

option button: A button in a dialog box that you click to perform a task or open another dialog box.

orphan: A single line of text at the start of a paragraph that appears at the very bottom of a page. Orphans sort of cheat the reader, because the reader can't tell how long the paragraph is until he or she turns the page. *See also* widow.

paste: To copy text or a graphic from the Clipboard to a document.

point: A unit for measuring type size. One point equals $1/72$ of an inch.

radio button: One of a set of two or more option buttons, only one of which can be selected. Radio buttons are round.

right-click: To click with the right mouse button.

save: To copy the data on-screen to the computer's hard disk. Data is not stored permanently until you save it.

scroll: To move through a document by using the scroll bars along the right side and bottom of the screen.

section: A part of a document. You cannot change page numbering schemes or margin sizes without creating a new section.

shortcut menu: A menu that appears when you right-click on-screen. Which shortcut menu appears depends on which part of the screen you click.

sort: To arrange the data in a table in a new way.

style: A format for headings, paragraphs, and other parts of a document. You can assign a new style by choosing one from the Style menu on the Formatting toolbar. Never to be confused with the term as used to describe a unique way of dressing.

taskbar: The bar along the bottom of the screen in Windows 95. The names of the applications that are running appear on buttons on the taskbar. Click a button to switch to another application.

template: A collection of styles you can choose from for formatting documents. All the styles in a template appear in the Style menu on the Formatting toolbar. *See also* style.

toolbar: An assortment of buttons for performing tasks. Word offers 11 toolbars.

typeface: *See* font.

widow: A very short line, usually one word, that appears at the end of a paragraph. Widows create a lot of ugly white space across the page. *See also* orphan.

Index

Symbols

* (asterisk) wildcard, 128
+ (plus) Outline view icon, 122
... (ellipses)
  commands and, 10
  Outline view and, 122
? (question mark) wildcard, 128

A

aligning text, 55–56
Alt key, 8
  See also keyboard shortcuts
anchoring, 130–131
annotations, 160–161
  copying, 160
  defined, 160
  deleting, 161
  finding, 161
  viewing, 160
  writing, 160
arrow keys, 8, 137
asterisk (*) wildcard, 128
AutoCorrect, 97–99
  additional uses, 98–99
  defined, 197
  exceptions, 98
  settings, 97–98
AutoCorrect dialog box, 97–98
  Exceptions button, 98
  illustrated, 97
AutoCorrect Exceptions dialog box, 98
AutoFormat dialog box, 68–69
AutoText dialog box, 102
AutoText list, 102–103
  defined, 102
  entering text or graphics from, 103

B

backups, 184–187
  file, 185–186
  floppy disk, 184–185
  restoring, 186–187
  tape drive, 184–185
binding, making room for, 158
boldface, 54
  this book, 4
  See also italics; underlining
Bookmark dialog box, 96

bookmarks, 96–97
  deleting, 96–97
  going to, 96
  placing, 96
  viewing, 97
borders, paragraphs and graphics, 131–133
  options, 132
  See also frames
borders, tables, 135, 144–145
  drawing, 144–145
Borders toolbar, 132
  Button Border button, 145
  displaying, 132, 144
  illustrated, 144
  Line Style menu, 132, 144, 145
  Outside Border button, 132
  Shading menu, 132, 145
  Top Border button, 144
Break dialog box, 60
bulleted lists, 57–59
bullets, 57
Bullets and Numbering dialog box, 58–59
  Bulleted tab, 58
  Multilevel tab, 58
  Numbered tab, 58
busy cursor, 7

C

caps
  drop, 60–61
  small, 55
Caps Lock key, 8
Caption dialog box, 177
Caption Numbering dialog box, 177
captions, 176–178
case, changing, 20–22
Cell Height and Width dialog box
  Column tab, 143
  Row tab, 142–143
cells
  defined, 135, 197
  merging, 146
  selecting, 138
  splitting, 146
  See also tables
Change Case dialog box, 21
check boxes, 12, 197
clicking, 9, 197
clip art. *See* graphics
Clipboard, 23, 191, 197

Close button, 14, 16
  illustrated, 16
  using, 22, 25
colors, adding to text, 134
Columns dialog box, 75–76
  options, 75–76
  Preview box, 75
columns, document (newspaper-style),
      74–77
  border bars, 74–75
  creating, 74–75
  justifying, 77
  line between, 75
  number of, 75
  spacing between, 76
  width, 76
  See also rows
columns, table, 135–143
  AutoFit, 143
  deleting, 139
  inserting, 139
  moving, 140
  number of, 136
  selecting, 139
  shading, 143
  width, changing, 136, 142
  See also rows; tables
commands
  changing, 99–101
  editing, 11
  ellipses (...) and, 10
  issuing, 4
  underlined letters in, 4
  See also specific menus and commands
concordance files, 168–169
Confirm Password dialog box, 194
Control menu, 14
conventions, this book, 3–4
Convert Text to Table dialog box, 137
copying
  annotations, 160
  drag-and-drop, 23
  text, 22–23
  See also moving
Copying message box, 184–185
Create Data Source dialog box, 107
Create Labels dialog box, 91–92
cropping graphics, 155, 197
Cross-reference dialog box, 178–179
cross-references, 178–179
  creating, 178–179
  defined, 178
  index, 168
Ctrl key, 8
  See also keyboard shortcuts
cursors, 6–7
  defined, 6, 197
  types of, 7

Custom Button dialog box, 126
Customize dialog box, 100–102, 115–116
  Keyboard tab, 101
  Menus tab, 100
  Toolbar tab, 125
customizing toolbars, 124–125
customizing Word for Windows 95, 99–102
  keyboard shortcuts, 101–102
  menu commands, 99–101

D

dashes, 24
Data Form dialog box, 108
Database dialog box, 166, 167
  Get Data button, 166
  Insert Data button, 167
  Query Options button, 166
  Table AutoFormat button, 166
databases
  in documents, 166–168
  importing, 166–168
Delete key, 8, 24, 40
deleting
  annotations, 161
  bookmarks, 96–97
  columns, 139
  endnotes, 182
  field markers, 173
  footers, 40
  footnotes, 182
  frames, 153
  headers, 40
  macros, 117
  page breaks, 18
  page numbers, 37
  passwords, 194
  rows, 139
  subdocuments, 120
  text, 24
  toolbar buttons, 125
  toolbars, 124, 127
desktop publishing, 129–158
dialog boxes
  check boxes, 12, 197
  defined, 11, 198
  drop-down list, 12, 198
  filling in, 11–12
  radio buttons, 12, 199
  scroll list, 12
  tabs, 12
  See also specific dialog boxes
.doc file extension, 6, 41
documents
  annotating, 160–161
  binding, making room for in, 158
  closing, 22
  databases in, 166–168

defined, 6, 198
file extension for, 6
formatting, 61–69
grammar-checking, 30–31
heading numbering, 72
highlighting parts of, 190
hyphenating, 31–33
indexing, 168–173
information about, 188–189
inserting
  automatic information in, 111
  files in, 34
landscape, 157–158
line numbering, 73–74
linking, 112–115
list of, File menu, 39
main, 106
master, 117–121
merging, 106
moving around in, 34–35, 110–111
multiple, 49–50
names of, 41
newspaper-style columns, 74–77
opening, 38–39
  existing, 38
  new, 38–39
  second window, 50–51
previewing, 82–83
printing, 86–87
protecting from changes, 195–196
revisions, 173–176
saving, 6, 40–42
  for first time, 40–41
  under new name, 41–42
  worked on, 42
sections, 59–60
source, 106
spell-checking, 45–46
split screen, 51–52
views, 14, 48–49
window, 14
See also files; text
double-clicking, 9, 198
drag-and-drop, 23, 198
drawing, 147
  borders on tables, 144–145
Drawing toolbar, 147
  Borders button, 154
  Create Picture button, 154
  Insert Frame button, 154
  Text box button, 154
Drop Cap dialog box, 61
drop caps, 60–61
  creating, 61
  defined, 60
  sizing, 61
drop-down list, 12, 198

E

Edit menu
  AutoText command, 102, 103
  Bookmark command, 96, 179
  Clear command, 24
  Copy command, 22
  Cut command, 22
  Find command, 27
  Go To command, 35, 110, 161, 173
  Linked Document Object command, 115
  Links command, 114
  Paste command, 22
  Repeat commands, 127
  Replace command, 25
  Select All command, 134
  Undo command, 47
editing, 17–52
  commands, 11
  endnotes, 182
  footnotes, 182
  indexes, 173
ellipses (...)
  commands and, 10
  outline view and, 122
em dash, 24, 97
en dash, 24
End key, 8
endnotes
  defined, 179
  deleting, 182
  editing, 182
  inserting, 180–181
  moving, 182
  options, 181–182
  See also footnotes
Enter key, 8
Envelope Options dialog box, 84–85, 93
Envelopes and Labels dialog box, 83–84, 88–89
  Envelopes tab, 83–84, 93
  Labels tab, 88–89
envelopes, printing, 83–85
Esc key, 7
Explorer utility, 184
exporting files, 191

F

F keys. *See* function keys
Field dialog box, 111
Field Options dialog box, 111
fields
  defined, 107, 198
  inserting, 111
  in templates, 104
  names of, 107

file extensions
  defined, 41, 198
  .doc, 6, 41
  .wbk, 187
File menu
  Close command, 22
  document list, 39
  Exit command, 16, 25
  New command, 38, 67, 105, 118
  Open command, 10, 38, 187, 190
  Page Setup command, 73, 77, 157, 158
  Print command, 86, 93, 94
  Print Preview command, 76, 82, 86
  Properties command, 189
  Save As command, 41, 42, 104, 120, 186, 191
  Save command, 6, 40, 42, 51, 92
files
  concordance, 168–169
  exporting, 191
  finding, 187–188
  formats for, 191
  importing, 190–191
  inserting in documents, 34
  password-protected, 194
  restoring, 186–187
  saving, 6, 40–42
  See also documents; file extensions
Find dialog box, 27–28
finding
  annotations, 161
  files, 187–188
  text, 27–29
  wildcards and, 128
finding and replacing, 25–26
Font dialog box, 54–55, 57
  Character Spacing tab, 148
  Color menu, 134
  Default button, 57
  Effects area, 165
  illustrated, 54, 134
  Small Caps option, 55
  Strikethrough option, 54
  Subscript option, 55
  Superscript option, 55
  Underline settings, 55
fonts
  changing, 56–57
  defined, 56, 198
  points, 199
  printing, 93
  sizes, 57
footers
  defined, 39, 198
  deleting, 40
  margins, adjusting for, 78
  See also headers

Footnote and Endnote dialog box, 180–181
  illustrated, 180
  Numbering area, 180
  Options button, 181
footnotes
  defined, 179
  deleting, 182
  editing, 182
  inserting, 180–181
  moving, 182
  options, 181–182
  See also endnotes
Form Field dialog box, 104–105
form letters, 106–110
  generating, 106–110
  main document, 106
  source document, 106
  See also Mail Merge Helper
Format menu
  AutoFormat command, 68
  Borders and Shading command, 132
  Bullets and Numbering command, 59
  Change Case command, 21
  Columns command, 74, 75
  Drop Cap command, 61
  Font command, 54, 57, 134, 148, 165
  Frame command, 130, 151
  Heading Numbering command, 72
  Paragraph command, 14, 19, 56, 71, 77, 155
  Style command, 63, 66
  Style Gallery command, 67
  Tabs command, 80
Format Painter, 62
Format toolbar, 14, 54
  Alignment button, 55
  Bold button, 54
  Bullets button, 58
  Columns button, 74
  Decrease Indent button, 69, 70
  Format Painter button, 62
  Highlight button, 190
  Increase Indent button, 69, 70
  Italic button, 54
  Numbering button, 58
  Underline button, 54
formatting, 53–80
  automatic, 68–69
  documents, 61–69
  finding and replacing, 25–26
  with Format Painter, 62
  paragraph, 14–15
  styles and, 62–67
  tables, 143–145
  text, 53–80
forms, 103–105
  defined, 103
  functioning of, 103

into templates, 103–104
See also templates
Formula dialog box, 146–147
Frame dialog box, 130–131
  Horizontal area, 152
  illustrated, 151
  Size area, 152
  Text Wrapping area, 151
  Vertical area, 152–153
frames, 130–131, 132, 149–153
  changing, 150–153
  deleting, 153
  dotted lines, 150
  inserting, 149–150
  moving, 150–153
  selection handles, 150
  sizing, 150
  See also borders, paragraphs and
    graphics
function keys, 7, 198
  F1 (help), 29
  F4 (repeat), 127
  F7 (spelling), 45

G

Go To dialog box, 35, 110, 161, 173
  Enter Reviewer's Name box, 161
  Go to What menu, 110
  illustrated, 110, 161
  Next button, 161
  Previous button, 110, 161
Grammar Checker, 30–31
graphics
  anchoring, 130–131
  cropping, 155
  entering quickly, 102–103
  inserting, 153–155
  moving, 150
  printing, 93
  sizing, 150
  text inside, 154
gridlines, 135
gutter, 78, 198

H

hanging indents, 58, 70
Header and Footer toolbar, 39–40
Header Record Delimiters dialog box, 91
header row, 146, 167, 198
headers
  defined, 39, 198
  deleting, 40
  inserting, 39–40
  margins, adjusting for 78
  See also footers
Heading Numbering dialog box, 72

headings
  numbering, 72
  spacing between letters in, 148
Help, 29–30
  button, 29
  cursor, 7
  F1 key, 29
  mini-Help screen, 29
Help menu, 30
  About Microsoft Word command, 30
  Microsoft Word Help Topics command, 29
Help Topics dialog box, 29–30
  Answer Wizard tab, 30
  Contents tab, 29
  Find, 30
  getting to, 29
  Index tab, 29
hidden text, 165
highlighting, 190
Home key, 8
hot keys, 4, 198
hyphenating, 31–34
  automatic, 31–32
  manual, 32–33
  one paragraph, 33
  ragged right margin and, 31
  unhyphenating and, 33
Hyphenation dialog box, 31–32

I

icons
  plus, in Outline view, 122
  square, in Outline view, 122
  this book, 2–3
importing
  databases, 166–168
  files, 190–191
indent markers, 70–71
  first-line, 70
  illustrated, 70
  left, 70, 71
  right, 70, 71
indents, 69–71
  changing, 70
  defined, 69
  hanging, 70
  margins vs., 77
  ruler and, 70
Index and Tables dialog box
  Index tab, 169–170, 171–172
  Table of Contents tab, 163–164
  Table of Figures tab, 162–163
indexes, 168–173
  cross-references, 168
  editing, 173
  generating, 171–172

(continued)

indexes *(continued)*
  importance of, 168
  marking items in, 168–171
  terminology, 168
  updating, 173
Insert Data dialog box, 167
Insert File dialog box, 34
Insert key, 7
Insert menu
  Break command, 18, 60
  Caption command, 177
  Cross-reference command, 178
  Database command, 166
  Field command, 111
  File command, 34
  Footnote command, 180, 181
  Form Field command, 104
  Frame command, 130, 149, 150
  Index and Tables command, 161, 169
  Object command, 192
  Page Numbers command, 36
  Pictures command, 153
  Symbol command, 24, 46
Insert Picture dialog box, 153–154
Insert Subdocument dialog box, 119
Insert Table dialog box, 136–137
inserting
  automatic information, 111
  columns, in tables, 139
  the date or time, 111
  endnotes, 180–181
  fields, 111
  files, 34
  footnotes, 180–181
  frames, 149–150
  graphics, 153–155
  page numbers, 36
  rows, in tables, 139
  section breaks, 18, 60
  subdocuments, in master documents, 119
  symbols, 24, 46
insertion point, 7
italics, 54
  See also boldface; underlining

K

kerning, 148, 198
keyboard keys, 7–8
keyboard shortcuts, 3
  Alt+5, 139
  Alt+End, 137
  Alt+F4, 25
  Alt+F, 9
  Alt+Home, 137
  Alt+Page Up/Down, 137
  Alt+Shift+X, 170

  changing, 101–102
  Ctrl+1, 44
  Ctrl+2, 44
  Ctrl+A, 134
  Ctrl+Alt+hyphen, 99
  Ctrl+B, 54
  Ctrl+C, 22
  Ctrl+E, 55
  Ctrl+End, 35
  Ctrl+Enter, 18
  Ctrl+F6, 50
  Ctrl+F, 27
  Ctrl+G, 110
  Ctrl+H, 25
  Ctrl+Home, 35
  Ctrl+hyphen, 33, 77
  Ctrl+I, 54
  Ctrl+J, 55
  Ctrl+L, 55
  Ctrl+N, 38, 118, 168, 187, 190
  Ctrl+O, 10, 38
  Ctrl+P, 86, 94
  Ctrl+PgDn, 35
  Ctrl+PgUp, 34
  Ctrl+R, 55
  Ctrl+S, 40, 42, 92
  Ctrl+Shift+<, 57
  Ctrl+Shift+>, 57
  Ctrl+Shift+Enter, 76
  Ctrl+Shift+F5, 96
  Ctrl+U, 54
  Ctrl+V, 22
  Ctrl+X, 22
  Ctrl+Y, 127
  Ctrl+Z, 101
  Shift+Enter, 18, 77
  Shift+F3, 21
  Shift+F7, 26
  Shift+Tab, 105, 137

L

Label Options dialog box, 88–89, 91
labels
  generating, 89–92
  printing, 87–93
    for mass mailings, 89–93
    one at a time, 88–89
    options, 89
  saving, 92
  See also Mail Merge Helper
landscape documents, 157–158
leading
  defined, 47, 198
  symbols and, 47
line breaks, 18
Line Numbers dialog box, 73

lines
    breaking in wrong places, 94
    indenting, 69–71
    keeping together, 155–157
    numbering, 73–74
    selecting, 43
    spacing, 43–44
    See also paragraphs
links, 112–115
    automatic, 114
    breaking, 114
    creating, 112–113
    manual, 114
    saving as picture, 115
    updating, 113–114
Links dialog box, 114–115
lowercase, 20–21
See also case, changing

M

Macro dialog box, 115, 117
    Delete button, 117
    illustrated, 117
    Record button, 115
    Run button, 117
Macro Record toolbar, 116
macros, 115–117
    defined, 115
    deleting, 117
    recording, 115–116
    running, 116–117
    running from toolbars, menus, keyboard,
        115–116
Mail Merge Helper, 89
    Create button, 90, 106
    Get Data button, 90, 106
    illustrated, 91
    Merge button, 90, 108
    opening, 90
    using, 90–93
    See also form letters; labels
mailing lists, 89–90
    paragraph symbols and, 90
    See also Mail Merge Helper
main menu, 9
margins, 77–78
    changing, 77–78
    default settings, 78
    defined, 77, 199
    gutter, 78
    indents vs., 77
    mirror, 78
Mark Index Entry dialog box, 170–171
    Cross-reference option, 171
    Current Page option, 171
    Main Entry box, 170
    Page Number Format box, 171

    Page Range option, 171
    Subentry box, 170
    Sub-subentry box, 170
Master Document toolbar, 117
    Insert Subdocument button, 119, 120
    Lock button, 121
    Merge Subdocument button, 121
    Remove Subdocument button, 120
    Split Subdocument button, 121
Master Document view, 117
master documents, 117–121
    assembling documents, 118–120
    creating, 118
    defined, 117
    subdocuments, 117, 120–121
Maximize/Restore button, 14, 16
    illustrated, 16
    using, 50
menu bar, 14
menus
    changing, 99–101
    commands, 10
    defined, 9
    pull down, 9–10
    See also specific menus
Merge Dialog box, 92, 109–110
    illustrated, 92, 110
    options, 109–110
merging subdocuments, 120–121
mini-Help screen, 29
Minimize button, 14, 16
mirror margins, 78
Modify Numbered List dialog box, 59
Modify Style dialog box, 66–67, 164
mouse
    buttons, 9
    clicking, 9
    cursor, 7
    defined, 199
    using, 9
moving
    around in documents, 34–35, 110–111
    columns/rows, 140
    drag-and-drop, 23
    endnotes, 182
    footnotes, 182
    frames, 150–153
    graphics, 150
    subdocuments, 120
    text, 22–23
    See also copying

N

new document, opening, 38
New Style dialog box, 64–65
New Toolbar dialog box, 126
Normal view, 48

Note Options dialog box, 181–182
  All Endnotes tab, 181
  All Footnotes tab, 181
Num Lock key, 8
numbered lists, 57–59
numbering
  headings, 72
  lines, 73–74
  pages, 36–37

O

Object dialog box, 192
Open Data Source dialog box, 90, 166
Open dialog box
  Files of type box, 191
  for finding files, 187–188
  illustrated, 38
  options, 188
  Text Files option, 191
Open Index AutoMark dialog box, 170
opening
  existing documents, 38
  mailing lists for creating labels, 90
  Mail Merge Helper, 90
  new documents, 38–39
  password-protected files, 194
  second window, 50–51
  Style Gallery, 67
  templates, 105
  Thesaurus, 26
Options dialog box, 99
  AutoFormat tab, 57–58
  Edit tab, 23, 43
  General tab, 78, 196
  illustrated, 13
  Print tab, 93, 165
  Revisions tab, 174–175
  Save tab, 185–186, 193, 194
  Spelling tab, 45–46
  User Info tab, 85
  View tab, 20, 49, 97, 138, 165
orphans, 157, 199
Outline view, 110–111, 121–123
  defined, 49, 121
  illustrated, 122
  plus icon, 122
  square icon, 122
  text selection in, 122–123
  view options, 121–122

P

page breaks, 18–19
  deleting, 18
  inserting, 18
  paragraphs and, 19
  See also pages

Page Layout dialog box, 73
Page Layout view, 40, 61
  defined, 48
Page Number Format dialog box, 36–37
  Include Chapter Number options, 36–37
  Number Format options, 37
  Page Numbering options, 37
page numbering, 36–37
  deleting, 37
  options, 37
  See also pages
Page Numbers dialog box, 36
Page Setup dialog box
  Layout tab, 73–74
  Margins tab, 77–78, 158
  Paper Size tab, 85–86, 157
Page Up/Down keys, 8, 34
pages
  collate, 87
  printing odd/even, 87
  shrinking, 76
  text running off, 93
  See also page breaks
pagination, 155–157
  codes, 156
paper
  orientation, 157
  sizes, 85–86, 94
  source, 94
  See also printing
Paragraph Borders and Shading dialog box
  Borders tab, 132
  Shading tab, 133
Paragraph dialog box
  Indents and Spacing tab, 44, 71
  Text Flow tab, 19
    Pagination area, 155–156
    Widow/Orphan Control check box, 157
paragraph symbol, 15, 90
paragraphs, 14–15, 32–33
  defined, 14
  formatting, 14–15
  indenting, 69–71
  keeping together, 155–157
  page breaks and, 19
  selecting, 43
  See also lines
Password dialog box, 194, 195
passwords, 192–196
  deleting, 194
  keeping others from changing, 194–195
  protected file, opening, 194
  setting, 193
pasting
  defined, 199
  drag-and-drop, 23
  text, 22–23
  See also copying; moving

pictures. *See* graphics
plus (+) Outline view icon, 122
Print dialog box, 11, 86–87
    Collate option, 87
    illustrated, 94
    Name drop-down menu, 94
    Number of copies option, 87
    Print option, 87
    Print Range options, 86–87
    Print to file option, 87
    Print what option, 87
    Properties button, 94
Print Preview screen, 82–83
    buttons, 82–83
    illustrated, 82
printers, problem solving, 93–94
printing, 81–94
    collate, 87
    on different-sized paper, 85–86
    documents, 86–87
    envelope, 83–85
    fonts, 93
    graphics, 93
    labels, 87–93
        for mass mailings, 89–93
        one at a time, 88–89
        options, 89
    odd/even pages, 87
    previewing, 82–83
    See also paper
properties, 189
Properties dialog box
    Contents tab, 189
    Custom tab, 189
    General tab, 189
    Paper tab, 94
    Statistics tab, 189
    Summary tab, 189
Protect Document dialog box, 195–196

Q

question mark (?) wildcard, 128

R

radio buttons, 12, 199
ragged right margin, 31
Reapply Style dialog box, 66
Record Macro dialog box, 115–116
Replace dialog box, 25–26
Reset Toolbar dialog box, 125
Restore button. *See* Maximize/Restore
        button
Review AutoFormat Changes dialog box, 69
Review Revisions dialog box, 176
revision marks, 173–174

revisions, 173–176
    accepting/rejecting, 176
    marking, 174–175
Revisions dialog box, 174–176
    Accept All button, 176
    Compare Versions button, 175
    illustrated, 174
    Merge Revisions button, 175
    Options button, 174
    Reject All button, 176
    Review button, 176
right-click, 9, 199
    See also shortcut menus
rows
    deleting, 139
    header, 146, 167
    height, changing, 142–143
    inserting, 139
    moving, 140
    number of, 136
    selecting, 138
    shading, 143
    See also columns; tables
ruler, 14
    indents and, 70
    tabs, 80
    units of measurement, 78
    using, 78–79
    viewing, 19, 78

S

Save As dialog box, 6, 40–42
    File name text box, 41, 104, 120
    illustrated, 40, 42
    Save as type list, 41, 191
    Save button, 186
    Up One Level button, 41
saving
    automatic, 186–187
    defined, 199
    documents, 6, 40–42
        for first time, 40–41
        under new name, 41–42
        worked on, 42
    labels, 92
    options, 185–186
    templates, 105
screen
    full, 19
    illustrated, 13
    mini-Help, 29
    parts of, 14
    splitting, 51–52
scroll
    bar, 35
    box, 35
    defined, 199
    list, 12

searching. *See* finding; finding and replacing
secret messages (hidden text), 165
sections, 59–60
  creating, 59–60
  defined, 59, 199
security. *See* passwords
selecting
  cells, 138
  columns, 139
  rows, 138
  tables, 139
  text, 43
selection handles, 150
shading, 131–133
  columns/rows, 143
  options, 133
  table, 145
  See also tables
Shift key, 8
  See also keyboard shortcuts
shortcut keys. *See* keyboard shortcuts
shortcut menus
  Borders command, 132
  Copy command, 23
  Customize command, 124
  Cut command, 23, 140
  defined, 9, 10, 199
  Drawing command, 147, 154
  Open Document Link command, 115
  Paste command, 23, 140
  Toggle Field Codes command, 179
  toolbars on, 123
  Update Field command, 168, 173
  Update Link command, 113
Smart Cut and Paste, 23
Sort dialog box, 141
sorting
  defined, 199
  tables, 140–141
sound, 191–192
spacing
  headings between characters in, 148
  lines, 43–44
spell-checking, 45–46
  drawbacks to, 46
  options, 45–46
Spelling dialog box, 45–46
  AutoCorrect button, 98
Standard toolbar, 14
  Copy button, 22
  Cut button, 22
  Insert Table button, 136
  New button, 38, 118, 168
  Open button, 38, 187, 190
  Outline View button, 121
  Page Layout View button, 74
  Paste button, 22

  Print Preview button, 82
  Redo button, 127
  Save button, 40, 42, 92
  Show/Hide button, 165
  Spelling button, 45
  Undo button, 127
  View buttons, 14
  viewing, 19
  See also toolbars
starting Word 95, 15–16
status bar, 14
  MRK button, 174
  REC button, 115
strikethrough style, 54
Style dialog box, 164
  Apply button, 65
  illustrated, 65
  New button, 63
  Styles list, 65
Style Gallery, 67–68
  illustrated, 68
  opening, 67
  templates, 67
Style menu, 62–63
styles, 62–67
  applying, 65
  changing, 65–66
  creating, 63–65
  default, 62–63
  defined, 199
  keyboard shortcuts and, 64
  repeating, 127
  from Style Gallery, 67–68
  templates and, 64
  types of, 64
  See also formatting
subdocuments, 117
  inserting, 119
  locking, 121
  merging, 120–121
  moving, 120
  removing, 120
  renaming, 121
  splitting, 121
  unlocking, 121
  See also master documents
subscript, 55
superscript, 54
Symbol dialog box, 24, 46–47
  illustrated, 47
  Special Characters tab, 47
  Symbols tab, 46–47
symbols, 46–47
  leading and, 47
  paragraph, 15, 90
  tab, 79
  tall, 47

T

Tab key, 79
Table AutoFormat dialog box, 143–144,
     166–167
  Apply Special Formats To area, 167
  Formats to Apply area, 167
  Preview box, 166
Table menu, 135
  AutoFormat command, 143
  Cell Height and Width command, 142
  Convert Table command, 135
  Convert Text to Table command, 137
  Delete Columns command, 139
  Delete Rows command, 139
  Formula command, 146
  Gridlines command, 137
  Insert Columns command, 139
  Insert Rows command, 139
  Insert Table command, 136, 168
  Merge Cells command, 146
  Select Column command, 139
  Select Row command, 138
  Select Table command, 139
  Sort command, 140, 141
  Split Cells command, 146
  Split Table command, 146
table of contents, 163–165
  creating, 163
  leader, 164
  options, 164
  page numbers, 164
Table of Contents Options dialog box, 164
table of figures, 161–163
Table Wizard, 137
tables, 135–147
  borders, 135
  cells, 135, 146
  creating, 136–137
  entering text in, 137–138
  formatting, 143–145
  gridlines, 135
  header row, 135
  illustrated, 135
  layout, changing, 138–143
  math formulas in, 146–147
  merging/splitting, 146
  selecting, 139
  sorting information in, 140–141
  See also columns; rows
tabs, 79–80
  changing, 79
  chart, 79
  default, 79
  removing, 80
  ruler, 80
  symbols, 79

Tabs dialog box, 80
taskbar
  defined, 199
  Start button, 15
  switching applications with, 16
templates
  defined, 67, 200
  fields, 104
  forms into, 103–104
  opening, 105
  saving, 105
  style, 64
  Style Gallery, 67
  See also forms
text
  aligning, 55–56
  anchoring, 130–131
  centering, 55–56
  coloring, 134
  copying, 22–23
  deleting, 24
  entering, 102–105
  entering in tables, 137–138
  finding, 27–29
  finding/replacing, 25–26
  fonts, 56–57
  formatting, 53–80
  in graphics, 154
  hidden, 165
  hyphenating, 31–34
  justifying, 55–56
  lowercase, 20–21
  moving, 22–23
  pasting, 22–23
  selecting, 43
  selecting in Outline view, 122–123
  uppercase, 20–21
  zooming, 52
  See also documents
text frames, 61
Thesaurus, 26–27
  illustrated, 27
  opening, 26
  options, 27
Tip of the Day, 196
TipWizard, 196
title bar, 14
  defined, 6
toolbars
  Borders, 132, 144–145
  buttons
    adding, 126–127
    changing, 124–125
    deleting, 125
    list of, 126
    moving, 125

(continued)

toolbars *(continued)*
 symbol, 127
 text, 127
 creating, 126–127
 customizing, 124–125
 defined, 200
 deleting, 124, 127
 displaying, 123–124
 Drawing, 147, 154
 Format, 14, 54, 54–55, 58, 62, 69, 70, 74
 Header and Footer, 39–40
 illustrated, 124
 Macro Record, 116
 Master Document, 117, 119–121
 positioning, 123
 rearranging, 123–127
 on shortcut menu, 123
 sizing, 124
 Standard, 14, 22, 38, 45, 100, 118, 121
Toolbars dialog box, 19, 123
Tools menu
 AutoCorrect command, 97, 98
 Customize command, 100, 101, 124
 Envelopes and Labels command, 83, 88, 93
 Grammar command, 31
 Hyphenation command, 31, 32
 Language command, 46
 Macro button, 115, 117
 Mail Merge command, 90, 106
 Options command, 12, 20, 23, 43, 45, 49, 57, 78, 138, 165, 185, 193, 194
 Protect Document command, 192, 195
 Revisions command, 173, 174, 188
 Spelling command, 45
 Thesaurus command, 26
 Unprotect command, 196
typos, correcting, 97–99

U

underlining, 54, 55
 See also boldface; italics
undoing actions, 47–48
uppercase, 20–21

V

video clips, 191–192
View menu
 Full Screen command, 19
 Header and Footer command, 37, 39, 40
 Master Document command, 118, 120
 Normal command, 48, 180
 Outline command, 49, 121
 Page Layout command, 48, 74
 Ruler command, 19, 78
 Toolbars command, 19, 123, 125, 126
views, 14, 48–49
 Draft Font, 49
 Master Document, 117
 Normal, 48
 Outline, 49, 110–111, 121–123
 Page Layout, 40, 48, 61

W

.wbk file extension, 187
widows, 157, 200
wildcards, 128
Window menu
 Arrange All command, 50, 169
 document list, 49–50, 51
 New Window command, 50
 Remove Split command, 52
 Split command, 51
Windows 95, 16
 Explorer, 184
 switching applications with, 16
Windows 95 For Dummies, 16, 185, 188
windows
 opening second, 50–51
 splitting, 51–52
Word 95
 customizing, 99–102
 exiting, 16, 25
 screen, 13–14
 starting, 15–16
 tips for learning, 196
 window, sizing, 16
Word For Windows 95 For Dummies, 166
Word For Windows 95 For Dummies Quick Reference
 contents, 2
 conventions, 3–4
 feedback, 4
 how to use, 1
 icons, 2–3
words
 double-clicking, 62
 selecting, 43

Z

Zoom control box, 52
zooming, 52